RADICAL LOVE

From Separation to Connection with the
Earth, Each Other, and Ourselves

SATISH KUMAR

PARALLAX PRESS
BERKELEY, CALIFORNIA

Parallax Press
2236B Sixth Street
Berkeley, CA 94710
parallax.org

Parallax Press is the publishing division of
Plum Village Community of Engaged Buddhism, Inc.

Cover design by Jess Morphew
Cover art © iStock/ Getty Image Plus / Ju-Ju
Text design by Maureen Forys, Happenstance Type-O-Rama
Author photograph by Geoff Dalglish

Printed on recycled paper in the United States of America

Library of Congress Cataloging-in-Publication Data

Names: Satish Kumar, 1936– author.
Title: Radical love : from separation to connection with the Earth, each
    other, and ourselves / Satish Kumar.
Description: Berkeley, California : Parallax Press, 2023. | Summary:
    "Lessons from a life of activism and mindfulness for navigating social,
    political, and ecological crises"— Provided by publisher.
Identifiers: LCCN 2022040389 (print) | LCCN 2022040390 (ebook) | ISBN
    9781952692352 (trade paperback) | ISBN 9781952692369 (ebook)
Subjects: LCSH: Love—Philosophy. | Biopolitics. | Human ecology—Religious
    aspects. | Environmentalism--Religious aspects. | Mindfulness
    (Psychology)
Classification: LCC BD436 .S275 2023 (print) | LCC BD436 (ebook) | DDC
    128/.46—dc23/eng/20221011
LC record available at *https://lccn.loc.gov/2022040389*
LC ebook record available at *https://lccn.loc.gov/2022040390*

1 2 3 4 5 / 27 26 25 24 23

All good thoughts,
words, and actions are
threaded with love!

To Vinoba Bhave

Be silently
drawn by
the stronger
pull of what
you really love.

—RUMI

CONTENTS

Introduction: Radical Love in a Time of Crisis

PART ONE · *Love Is All*

PART TWO · *Radical Love Globally*

INTRODUCTION

Radical Love in
a Time of Crisis

In every crisis take the higher path,
the path of compassion, courage, and love.

—AMIT RAY

Gravity and love are two aspects of a single reality. They are the organizing principles of our precious planet and our amazing universe. Gravity holds dominion over the physical, our outer world. Love holds dominion over the metaphysical, our inner world. Gravity sustains our material existence, while love nourishes our spiritual existence. Gravity is to the body what love is to the heart, soul, and consciousness. Gravity relates to what can be measured, while love relates to what can be imagined. Gravity sustains matter; love gives it meaning. In the end, everything is held together by love.

Love is difficult to define but each of us has a sense, deep in our hearts, what it means. For me, love is the source of all positive and creative relationships. Love provides a solid foundation for family, friendship, fellowship, community, and camaraderie. Love gives birth to compassion, kindness, caring, courtesy, and cooperation. Out of love grows humanity, humility, hospitality, and harmony.

A lack of love leads to war, conflict, competition, exploitation, domination, and subjugation of people and of Nature. Militarism, the arms race, insecurity, and rivalry of all kinds arise wherever there is no love. When there is no love, then there is poverty, inequality, injustice, racial segregation, and caste or class discrimination. The dark clouds of narrow nationalism, wretched racism, and demeaning sexism are all dispelled by the light of love. In love, we find the end of separation and isolation. In love, there is the beginning of connection and communication. Love creates union and communion.

I have found that whatever the problem, love is the only solution. Whatever the question, love is the perfect answer. The pathologies of pride, greed, anger, and fear can be treated with the healing power of love. Love is the medicine for an excess of ego and anxiety, for the disease of depression and despair. Life without love is like a well without the water, a body without the soul, or words without meaning. The true purpose of life is to love. When I exist in love, I move from greed to gratitude, from ownership to relationship, from glamour to grace, and from attachment to engagement.

I have personally been blessed and graced with unconditional, unlimited love from countless people throughout my life. All parts of my body, mind, and spirit have been nurtured by this abundance of love. My beloved life companion, June, has been a fountain of love these past fifty years. We met in the crypt of St. Martin-in-the-Fields in Trafalgar Square in London, in 1971. I fell in love at the very first sight. I was on a short visit to Europe with a return ticket in my bag. After meeting June, I canceled the ticket, gave up my life in India, and settled with June in London. We read poetry together, edited together, gardened together, cooked together, and walked together. Together with June, love in my life became a living reality.

All great teachers and social reformers from ancient times to our own age have one common theme, the theme of love. From the Buddha to Jesus Christ, from Mahavira to Mohammed, from Lao Tzu to the Dalai Lama, from Mother Theresa to Martin Luther King, from Mahatma Gandhi to Nelson Mandela, and from Joan Baez to John Lennon, they all have encapsulated their teachings in one word: Love.

Love is more than a religious or a spiritual ideal. Love is a source of nourishment to the human imagination. Great poets and painters have always been inspired by the common narrative that is love. Shakespeare explored his passion in 154 sonnets, not to mention the countless ways he articulated the enduring power of love in his plays. From Tolstoy to Tagore, from Goethe to Goya, from Pushkin to Picasso, from Blake to Botticelli, from Rumi to Ruskin, the list of writers, poets, and artists who have been inspired and fueled by love is endless. Be it love of nature, love of a humanity, or love of God, love itself is the seed out of which the trees of literature and art have grown. It is love that feeds us at the best of times and the worst of times. And humanity is facing a time in which our very existence is under threat, a time in which love can make all the difference.

⏶

The year 2020 will be remembered as the year of COVID-19—the year of social distancing, lockdowns, and staying indoors even when the sun was shining, the flowers were flourishing, and the birds were singing their sweet songs. I took that time of quarantine, or self-isolation, as a blessing: a time for spiritual retreat and for reflection. I read Rumi and Hafiz. I read Shakespeare's sonnets. I read Rabindranath Tagore. I meditated upon the word *quarantine*, and its association with Lent. I learned that, originally, *quarantine* referred to the period of forty days Jesus Christ spent fasting in the desert.

Despite the opportunity for quiet reflection, I was overwhelmed to see so much suffering in the world, engulfed in an unprecedented crisis. In 2020 I was eighty-three years old, and I had never experienced such a drastic and dreadful situation in my entire life. Being in this crisis was worse than being in a state of war, which I have experienced. Wars are initiated by humans and can be controlled or ended by humans. But COVID-19 was a show of Nature's power, far beyond human control. Many people believe that through science and technology we can conquer Nature. But through a novel coronavirus, Nature has made abundantly clear that any talk of humans conquering her is sheer human arrogance. COVID-19 reminded us in no uncertain terms about the reality of human vulnerability.

Human desire to conquer Nature comes from the belief that humans are separate from Nature, that, in fact, we enjoy a superior power. This dualistic thinking is at the root of our inability to deal with many of the natural upheavals we face currently, such as forest fires, floods, global warming, and pandemics. We seem to believe that one way or the other we will find technological solutions to subjugate Nature and make her subservient. Rather than looking at the root causes of COVID-19, governments, industrialists, and scientists have taken refuge in looking for vaccines to avoid the disease. While vaccines may be a temporary solution, we need to think and act intelligently, and with greater wisdom. Rather than simply vaccinating to lessen the symptoms, we need to address the causes of the disease.

In answer to the question why the emergence of human infections of animal origin have increased in recent decades, Laura Spinney, a science journalist and author of *Pale Rider: The Spanish Flu of 1918 and How It Changed the World*, states that "the forces putting those viruses in our path are political and economic. They have to do with the rise of industrial-scale farming and the resulting marginalization of millions of smallholder farmers. They have been forced closer to uncultivable zones such as forests, where bats—reservoirs for coronavirus—lurk."

If we were to address the causes of COVID-19, rather than simply the symptoms, we would need to return to ecologically regenerative agriculture; to human-scale, local, low-carbon, and organic methods of farming. Food is not a commodity. Farming should not be motivated by financial profits. The purpose of farming is to feed people with healthy food. The end goal of agriculture is to produce nutritious food without depleting the health of the soil. Farming for profit directly or indirectly causes coronavirus!

To address the causes of COVID-19, we need to learn to live in harmony with Nature and within the laws of Nature. Humans are as much a part of Nature as any other form of life. Therefore, living in harmony with Nature is the urgent imperative of our time and the very first lesson humans, collectively, need to learn from the COVID-19 crisis. The second lesson is that all human actions have consequences. In the past hundred years, human activities have caused both diminishing biodiversity and increasing greenhouse gas emissions, producing climate change. Due to human activities the oceans are polluted by plastic, the soil is poisoned with artificial chemicals, and the rainforests are disappearing at an unprecedented speed. All these negative human activities are bound to result in disastrous consequences, such as floods, forest fires, and pandemics.

Modern civilization has inflicted untold suffering and damage in Nature. Now we are harvesting the consequences. We must change. We must move on to build a new paradigm. To restore health to the people, we must restore health to our precious planet Earth. Healing people and healing Nature is one and the same. With COVID-19, Nature sent us a strong message. We need to do everything we can to heal the Earth. Only positive actions will bring positive outcomes; this is the law of Karma.

The trinity of Market, Money, and Materialism has ruled the modern mind for far too long. Now is the time to slow down and, with humility, listen to the voice of Nature, the voice of the Earth. We need to replace this old trinity with a new one: the trinity of Soil, Soul, and Society. We need to welcome an Age of Ecology, an ecology of love.

Humanity needs to respond to this crisis positively and use it as an opportunity to redesign our agricultural, economic, and political systems, and our way of life. We need to learn to respect the place of wilderness. We need to learn to celebrate the abundant beauty and diversity of life. We need to realize that humans are an integral part of Nature. That what we do to Nature we do to ourselves. We are all interconnected and interrelated. We depend on each other. We are members of one Earth community and one Earthly family.

If this worldview becomes an integral part of our collective consciousness, and our love for the Earth becomes an organizing principle of mainstream society, then we will have different priorities and different values. Instead of economic growth at all costs, we will pursue the growth in the well-being of people and health of our planet. Poet and novelist Ben Okri wrote that "the real tragedy would be if we came through this pandemic without changing for the better. It would be as if all those deaths, all that suffering would mean nothing."

Going back to business as usual after this pandemic must not be an option. Before COVID-19, our society was already in the grips of the pandemic of a greed-virus. And due to this greed-virus, forests have died, lakes and rivers have died, species have died, children have died, the poor have died, war victims have died, refugees have died. Death and destruction on a vast scale have been the consequence of the greed-virus.

A crisis is also an opportunity. In the evolutionary process of Nature there have been many crises. Life has evolved through struggles over long periods of geological time. Perhaps this painful pandemic has come to give birth to a new consciousness, a consciousness of unity of life, a consciousness of caring and sharing, a consciousness of love.

We have already seen some wonderful signs of this new consciousness. Doctors and nurses around the world have put themselves in harm's way, giving their lives to serve the victims of the novel coronavirus. They were shining examples of selfless service. Here where I live in the United Kingdom, hundreds of thousands of ordinary people have volunteered to help the National Health Service. And countless volunteers in local communities have taken care of the old and sick. Throughout the world, governments have suspended fiscal rules to help individuals, communities, charities, and businesses. There has been an outpouring of solidarity, generosity, mutuality, and reciprocity. People have experienced a sense of deep belonging, profound gratitude, and unconditional love from many directions.

Many animosities were forgotten. Nations cooperated, helping and supporting each other in the spirit of mutual aid, rather than competing and fighting. Russia sent planeloads of medical equipment to Italy. China did the same for Serbia. If these spiritual qualities can be practiced in extraordinary times, then why not in ordinary times? If we can cooperate and collaborate, love and respect one another, in ordinary times, extraordinary conditions caused by human behavior are less likely to occur.

In addition to this outpouring of human spirit, we also saw a reduction of pollution and a partial recovery of natural environments. Dolphins were spotted in the canals of Venice and a clear, blue sky was experienced over the cities of Bombay and Beijing. Carbon emissions decreased and people and animals were able to breathe pure air again. If we can have a clean environment in extraordinary times, then why not in ordinary times?

Can we dare to hope that individuals, communities, and countries will learn to love each other, look after their environment, and create a new world order after this dreadful COVID-19 crisis has passed? As the Indian writer Arundhati Roy reminds us: "Historically pandemics have forced humans to break with the past and imagine their world anew. COVID-19 is no different. It is a portal, a gateway between one world and the next."

This experience should give us the confidence and courage to take bold actions to safeguard the health of Nature and the biosphere. We must remember that we are sitting on the branch of Nature. If we cut the branch upon which we are sitting, we are bound to fall. As we move beyond COVID-19, let us act together to care for the planet and for its people.

I am aware of the obstacles. There are corporations and companies, governments and businesses who have vested interests in the status quo. Social and environmental activists have been working for many years, warning of impending crises, but it seems too often as if no one is listening. For more than forty years I edited *Resurgence & Ecologist,* a British bimonthly magazine covering environmental issues, engaged activism, philosophy, arts, and ethical living. The message of *Resurgence* is to love: love yourself, love people, love planet, love nature. Its articles are underpinned by the spirit of love, urging social and environmental activists to shed their fear of doom and gloom and, instead, to act out of love. Act to uphold beauty and integrity. Activism is a journey and not a destination.

Love is an expression of our spirituality, our imagination, and our way of life. But love is also a practical and ecological imperative. My friend Deepak Chopra once said to me that the environment and nature are our extended bodies. The air is our breath, and the rivers and waters our circulation; if we don't pay attention to our ecological self then we risk extinction. So it follows, apart from anything else, that love of our natural environment is a survival imperative.

♡

From my mother, Anchi, to my beloved wife, June, from Mahatma Gandhi to my mentor Vinoba Bhave, and from my fellow ecowarriors to the many contributors to *Resurgence,*

I have learned and received an abundance of love. My soul has been soaked by a cool monsoon of love. What follows is a distillation of these teachings and experiences, as I have understood them. I humbly offer this book to you, my readers, with all my love.

SATISH KUMAR

PART ONE

Love Is All

Love does not dominate; it cultivates.

—GOETHE

1

A Monsoon of Love

*If I have all faith so as to remove mountains
but do not have love, I am nothing.*

1 CORINTHIANS 13:2

Life is a landscape of love, and love is the celebration of life. Love is the means and love is the end. Love is our path and it is our destination. Love is the goal. Love is a way of being. Love is a way of life. There is no way to love: love is the way.

Falling in love is not a one-day event; it is an everyday event. When we are in love we are in love all the time. We are in love every moment. The moment we wake up, we fall in love with each other and with life itself. Love never ends. Love endures. We are forever spellbound by the mystery of love. It is love for the sake of loving. There is no other motivation. Love is not logic, love is pure magic. Love is pure poetry, and pure pleasure.

Love is sacred. Love is unlimited and unconditional. Allow yourself to be swept away by the force of love. True love is to love even when your beloved is less than perfect. It is easy to love someone who is good and thought to be perfect. But true love is to love even those who may not be so good. To love is to be free from criticizing, complaining, and comparing. To practice universal love is to recognize that those who behave badly do so because they have not been loved. The American poet W. H. Auden goes even farther when he says that "those to whom evil is done do evil in return." Those who are loved, love in return. Let us create a monsoon of love and nourish all living beings. Only through the act of loving can we teach others how to love.

When Christ said, "Love your enemy," he did not say it lightly. He believed *amor vincit omnia:* love conquers all. By way of love, enemies become friends. Love keeps no record of wrongdoings. Love is not a path for the faint-hearted. Love requires courage, courage to turn the other cheek. To love is to be brave. Sing the song of love and all your worries and miseries will evaporate! Live in the ecstasy of love. Be sustained by love.

Love is the acceptance of oneself as one is, and acceptance of others as they are. Acceptance without expectation, without judgment, and without qualification is love. Free of expectations, love encounters no disappointment. Love is to accept bitter with sweet, dark with light, pain with pleasure—all with equanimity. The moment we bring love into our hearts, we transform illusion into imagination, and duality into unity. We transcend likes and dislikes and enter into the celebration of life as it is. When we drink the sweet nectar of love, there is a transformation, as expressed by the Sufi poet Jalal ud-Din Rumi:

> By love, the bitter becomes sweet;
> By love, copper becomes gold;
> By love, the dregs become clear;
> By love, pain becomes healing.

This is the transformative power of love. To love is to see God, because God is love and love is God. Love is the greatest religion on earth. Love is majestic and magnificent. Where there is love, there is hope. So love and rejoice.

Where do we begin our journey of love? With ourselves. Christ said, "Love your neighbor as yourself." The word *yourself* is the key. As you love yourself, love others. The "others" are only an extension of yourself. Loving your "self" is not selfish! If you cannot love yourself, how can you love someone else, and why should you expect someone else to love you?

Accepting yourself as you are and loving yourself for being who you are is a prerequisite for loving others as they are and who they are. We are made of each other.

Lovers take no offense and give no offense. Lovers have no enemies. Animosity is a consequence of hate, while friendship is the consequence of love. As bees love flowers and produce honey, lovers love each other and produce happiness. Love is the purpose of life and through love we find the meaning of life.

Rumi also said, "Your task is not to seek for love but merely to seek and find all the barriers within yourself that you have built against love." To live is to love, and to love is to risk. We risk being hurt, and we risk the possibility of not being loved in return. Do not wish to have a lover; simply be a lover. Having a lover is the inevitable result of being a lover.

Love awakens the soul, love nourishes the heart, love brings joy to our lives. Love is the most beautiful mantra of the mind. The balm of love heals all wounds, the wounds of anger and anxiety, fear and resentment.

Love of oneself—love of others—love of Nature is a continuum. Love is as natural to us as breathing.

All-embracing love manifests through many forms such as philology: love of learning; philosophy: love of wisdom; and philanthropy: love of people.

More intimately we experience erotic love. How beautiful it is to fall in love and be in the embrace of one's beloved! "I love you" can be the most powerful and beautiful sentence in the English language. We can and we should fall in love every day, even with the same beloved. In loving one we love all. Falling in love is a miracle. We are born thanks to the act of making love. Every one of us is a love child. There is no original sin; only original love.

Love takes us beyond reason, beyond intellect, and beyond description. Poets, artists, and mystics experience the ecstasy of romantic love physically, emotionally, imaginatively, and spiritually. Romantic poetry and art celebrate our heart connections with each other, with nature, and with humans. Love brings us to a place beyond right and wrong, a place of magnanimity and generosity. This is deep love of life. All we need is love because love is all and everything. Love is the answer. What is your question?

2

Love for All

Whenever you have truth, it must be given with love,
or the message and the messenger will be rejected.

—MAHATMA GANDHI

Once we open the doors of our hearts, we can let our love flow at a social, political, and ecological level. In my life, Mahatma Gandhi has been the profoundest influence to demonstrate the connection between intimate love and ultimate love, personal love and political love. Quite simply, he alludes to what we all must do when he states, "I offer you love."

Mahatma Gandhi was a champion of Radical Love. For him, love should permeate every aspect of our lives. All human activities should be informed by love. Love should be the organizing principle of individual lives, as well as of the whole of society. For Gandhi, love had no borders and no boundaries, no limits and no conditions. He said, "Where there is love there is life, and where there is love there is light."

Love as a basis of personal relationships has been accepted and advocated by many. All religions and most philosophical traditions preach and promote love as a foundation for personal behavior. But for Mahatma Gandhi, love should also be the motivation behind political policies, economic decisions, and business behaviors.

The practice of love among friends and family members is good but not in itself sufficient. Love has to come out of the confinements of homes, temples, and monasteries. Love should be practiced in the corridors of political power and in the marketplace, as well.

All our activities of agriculture, education, medicine, arts, and crafts should emerge from the foundation of love. All our work should be "love made visible." Teachers should teach not just to earn money, but because they love children and love teaching. Earning a living is a means to an end. The true purpose is to serve children. Similarly, doctors should practice medicine because they love to heal the sick, farmers should produce food because they love to feed the hungry, politicians should go into politics because they love to serve the people, and traders should engage in business because they love to meet the needs of their communities. Every profession needs a purpose.

To bring love into every sphere of society, Mahatma Gandhi developed the concept of Sarvodaya. This word has many meanings, including the well-being of all, love for all, and the happiness of all. Here "all" refers to all sentient beings, harmony at all levels.

Political philosophies like utilitarianism, socialism, and capitalism see human life above all other forms of life. And since, according to these views, human life is superior to the life of plants, animals, and oceans, humans are accorded the right to control them, exploit them, and use them as they wish. This anthropocentrism is contrary to the Gandhian philosophy of nonviolence and love, which is the foundation of Sarvodaya. The Mahatma believed that the value of other-than-human life should not be measured in terms of its usefulness to humans, because all life has intrinsic value. Therefore, reverence for all life is the fundamental principle of Sarvodaya.

Mahatma Gandhi rejected the utilitarian idea of the maximum good of the maximum number. Political and economic policies should be designed for the good of all, and not just for the majority. Political and social philosophy must respect the dignity of all life and not accord higher status to any one form of life. This includes human life and other-than-human life. We must love animal life, plant life, and every other form of life. Pollution of oceans and rivers with agrochemicals and plastic is violence to our waters. Contamination of the air with excessive carbon emissions and greenhouse gases shows a similar lack of love for the planet. Destruction of forests, cruelty to animals in factory farms, and the poisoning of soil with herbicides and insecticides are a consequence of an absence of love. Diminishing biodiversity is the result of diminishing kindness and compassion.

The holistic philosophy of Sarvodaya insists on changing human attitudes, human hearts, and human relationships with Nature as our guide. Our perspective needs to be based in the unity of life rather than the separation and dualism between human life and other-than-human life. An inner transformation is the prerequisite for changing human behavior.

According to the science of evolution, all life has evolved from the same source, from the same single origin. Oceans, forests, and animals are the ancestors of humankind. All living beings are made of the same basic five elements: earth, air, fire, water, and space.

Sarvodaya moves away from the story of separation and embraces a story of relationship, acknowledging we are all connected. Unity and diversity are complementary. Evolution is a journey from unity to diversity, and not a descent from unity to separation, and dualism. Diversity is not division. Diversity is the celebration of unity. All forms of diversity are interrelated through the intricate web of life. Through love of life, love of the Earth, and love of Nature, we take care of all life on the planet, without discrimination, without judgment, and without exception.

The mind-set that divides humans from Nature is the same that divides one group of humans from another group of humans. We divide people in the name of caste, class, nationality, politics, gender, race, religion, and lifestyle. We begin to put one group above another. We turn human diversity into human division. Such division leads to competition, conflict, and war. We devise our politics in the interest of one group rather than another. National interest of one country is seen to be conflicting with the interest of another. Class conflict leads to class war. The welfare of the working class is perceived to be contrary to the welfare of the bosses. All this is a consequence of separational and dualistic political philosophies.

Sarvodaya perceives the clash of interest among humans to be the result of the conditioning of our minds. In the greater scheme of things, all humans have a common interest. That common ground can be found in love. All people wish to be happy, healthy, and in harmony with each other and with the planet. Therefore, with a consciousness based in love, we share our happiness and well-being with others. We care for each other, and we care for the Earth. We design our policies to serve the interest of all, without exception. The principles of Sarvodaya suggest that we should love even those with whom we disagree. Love without borders and love without frontiers! Love has more power to win the hearts and minds than any number of bombs and weapons. As Gandhi taught us, we "conquer with love."

How do we talk about "all" without it seeming too broad and vague? Where do we start in our political decision making? Mahatma Gandhi answered these questions too. He said that, when making a policy decision and allotting funds from the governmental budget, we must ask who will benefit from the decisions we make. If a decision is going to benefit the poorest of the poor, the weakest of the weak, and the most deprived members of the society first, then that decision reflects love for all. Gandhi rejected the trickle-down theory of economic decision making. The economics and politics of love must be reflected in urgent and immediate action to end social injustice and the exploitation of the disadvantaged.

In terms of love for the whole planet, Mahatma Gandhi also had a simple formula. If human activities produce waste and pollution of the air, water, and soil, or inflict pain and suffering on animals, then those activities are contrary to our love of the Earth. Moreover, humans need to practice humility. Instead of exploiting natural resources to satisfy all our cravings, greed, extravagance, and desires, we need to take from Nature only enough to meet our genuine needs, and to do so with gratitude. Gandhi said, "The Earth provides enough for everybody's need but not enough for anybody's greed." Nature is not merely a resource for the economy; Nature is the source of life. Love for the Earth in practical terms means caring for our planet.

This is not simply a lofty ideal. It is pragmatic, and practical politics. It has been proven again and again that politics of separation, division, conflict, and competition are stressful, wasteful, and counterproductive. Politics that serve the interest of one group against another, or the interest of humans against Nature, have been tried and have failed repeatedly. Mahatma Gandhi believed that "power based on love is a thousand times more effective and permanent than the one derived from fear of punishment." He asks us to give the politics of love a chance.

The ideal of love is often considered to be a spiritual ideal, but for Gandhi there was no division between the practical and the spiritual. Solutions to our environmental problems, personal unhappiness, social divisions, economic inequality, international conflicts, racial discrimination, and any number of other pressing issues lie in one great idea—Sarvodaya: Love for all.

3

Unity

Those who experience the unity of life
see themselves in all beings,
and all beings in themselves.

—THE BUDDHA

Separation is the dominant story of our time. First and fore-most, separation is the separation of humans from Nature. We have come to think that Nature is out *there.* The hills, rivers, oceans, forests, animals, and birds are Nature. And all these parts of Nature are there to serve human needs. The purpose of science, technology, industry, and the econ-omy has been to conquer Nature and make her useful. She is subject to human need and even human greed. We can do to Nature what we like; we can cut down the rainforests, overfish the oceans, slaughter animals in abattoirs, poison the soil with chemicals, and kill wild creatures in the pur-suit of pleasure, power, and entertainment. According to this narrative, Nature is soulless; she has no spirit, no intelligence, no memory. Nature is inanimate. Nature is a machine.

The word *nature* simply means birth. Whatever is born is of Nature. When a mother is pregnant, she goes for a prenatal check. After the birth, she has a postnatal check. *Natal, nature, native*—all these words come from the same root. Humans are born of seed. Therefore, we are as much part of nature as trees, tigers, and turtles. Nature does not belong to us; we belong to Nature.

A new story is emerging. This is the story of Unity. In this story, we are all members of one Earth community. Aldo Leopold called it the "biotic community." All species, humans, and other-than-humans are sustained by the same elements of existence. We all breathe the same air, drink the same water, warm ourselves by the same sun, and feed ourselves from the same soil. How can we call ourselves separate from Nature? How can we consider ourselves as the masters of Nature?

Indigenous cultures talked about Mother Earth and Father Sky. They considered four-legged and two-winged creatures as their brothers and sisters, members of one Earthly family. Some of us live on the ground, others fly in the sky, and still others swim in the water, but ultimately the whole of life is one, manifesting in millions of shapes, forms, and functions. Diversity is the dance of one life force. Unity celebrates itself in the diversity of life. We are all connected, we are all related. We are an integral part of Nature. The Earth is our common home.

The old story of separation has infected the whole of human relationships. In the name of nationality or religion, under the cloak of color or race, we have built the great walls of narrow self-interest that separate one nation from another, one religion from another. The American national interest conflicts with the national interest of Russia. India and Pakistan, China and Japan, and many other conflicting nations see their national interests at odds with each other. We have forgotten the fundamental truth that before we are Americans or Russians, Israelis or Palestinians, Hindus or Muslims, Shias or Sunnis, Catholics or Protestants, Blacks or whites, we are members of one human tribe. Whatever our nationality or religion, we are all humans. Under our skin we all have the same blood flowing. At a quantum level, we are all protons and photons.

The new story is the story of radical pluralism. It is wonderful to have diversity of cultures and colors, nationalities and religions, faiths and philosophies. It would be extremely boring if seven billion humans of this Earth had only one language or one religion or one political system. Evolution favors diversity—biodiversity, religious and cultural diversity, political and economic diversity, diversity of truths and tongues. Let a thousand flowers bloom and let a million minds be free. The Earth is abundant. There is enough for everybody to share and celebrate. There is no need to fear and fight. Let us replace the old story of narrow national interest with this new story of common human interest. Let us replace the old story of separation with the new story of unity, of re-union. Let us transform our divisions into diversity and let us engage in dialogues over our differences. Ultimately there is only one Earth, only one humanity, and only one future. As E. M. Forster said: "Only connect … and human love will be seen at its height. Live in fragments no longer."

We can choose to perceive diversity as division or as a celebration of unity. We can look at the world and see it whole and perceive it as a network of relationships, or we can perceive the world as a collection of fragmented and disconnected entities fighting each other. In the view of Thomas Berry, an eco-theologian from the U.S., "the universe is not a collection of objects, it is a communion of subjects." All living beings, humans and other-than-humans belong to one great Tree of Life!

The mind, tired of divisions and conflicts, seeks to create a world of uniformity. At a global level, we have begun to see uniform architecture, uniform foods, drinks, and clothes. Franchised chain shops and restaurants are selling the same mass-produced goods and foods from New York to New Delhi, and from Beijing to Berlin. This uniformity is anything but unity.

We need to remind ourselves of the simple truth that wars, terrorism, climate change, poverty, and other major human problems are merely symptoms of the deep-rooted disease of our separation from Nature and our disconnection from our human community. Unless we address the root causes of our ecological and social crises, we are not going to be able to minimize or mitigate the pain of poverty, the agony of wars, and the distress caused by climate change. By embracing a new story of unity, we shift from our anthropocentric worldview to an ecocentric worldview; we move from self-interest to common interest, discovering unity in diversity.

Meditation on the Unity of Life

Left palm represents the self; right palm represents
   the world.

I bring my two palms together and by doing so I
   unite myself with the world.

I bow to sacred life, sacred Earth, sacred universe,
   sacred cosmos.

I bow to sacred soil, sacred air, sacred fire, sacred
   water, sacred space.

I see all beings in me and myself in all beings.

I see the whole universe in me and myself in the
   whole universe.

I am a microcosm of the macrocosm.

I am made of earth, air, fire, and water.

The cosmos is my country, Earth my home, Nature
   my nationality, and love my religion.

All living beings are sustained by the same breath of
   life, flow of water, warmth of fire, and solidity
   of soil.

Thus, we are all connected, we are all related, we are
   interbeings.

We share a single origin.

Unity and diversity dance together.

All our thriving is mutual.

I celebrate mutuality, reciprocity, and relationship.

When separation and division end, suffering also ceases.

I go beyond right and wrong, beyond good and bad.
I bow to the unity of life. I bow to the diversity of
   forms.
I breathe in and I breathe out.
I smile, I relax, and I let go.
I let go of all expectation, attachment, and anxiety.
I let go of all worry, fear, and anger.
I let go of ego.
I breathe in. I breathe out.
I smile, relax, and let go.
I am at home. I am at home. We are at home.

4

Diversity

I have decided to stick to love;
hate is too great a burden to bear.

—MARTIN LUTHER KING JR.

Breathe in gently and breathe out gently. And when you breathe in and breathe out, remember that we are all breathing the same air. All of humanity is breathing and sharing the same air. And the same is true of life beyond humanity: animals, plants, and minerals. All life is sustained by the same breath. With that sense of unity of life and connection with the whole, we breathe in and we breathe out, mindfully and heartfully. And we enjoy the life-sustaining breath without which we cannot survive.

When we breathe together, we think of millions of life forms. Diversity is the key to a healthy humanity and thus key to a new paradigm and a new civilization. Evolution favors diversity. In the beginning of time as we know it—at the instance of the Big Bang—there was no diversity at all. There was gas, and eventually water. And then, over billions of years of evolution, millions of different species emerged: plants and animals, fungi and bacteria. Biodiversity is a necessity for the flourishing of life. All life. But sadly, in pursuit of economic growth, we have forgotten our sacred responsibility to maintain biodiversity.

We have become confused. All our efforts are devoted to economic growth. The overwhelming majority of human beings has become an instrument of economic growth. Nature too has become an instrument of economic growth, a resource to be exploited for the purpose of making profit. When we look at Nature as a resource for the economy, then Nature's only value is how useful it is for the interest of human production and consumption of goods and services. We are treating Nature as a machine, as a utility. And so, we measure its value in terms of money. We sacrifice wildlife and wildlands for the sake of the economy. The result is that we are diminishing biodiversity in every sphere and on every level at an alarming rate.

It is comforting to know that this industrial paradigm— economy over ecology—is only a couple of hundred years old. Our indigenous brothers and sisters have lived in harmony with Nature for thousands of years. They know that Nature is not an economic means. Nature is not a resource for the economy. Nature is a source of life. Our planet is a sacred source of life, a living organism. The Earth is the common home for humans and all the other living species. In our new story, economy is a subset of ecology.

I firmly believe in human rights, but we need to go one step farther. We must say that nature also has rights. Rights of Nature go hand in hand with human rights. This interconnectedness, interdependence, and interrelationship need to be recognized and acknowledged. The rights of Nature must be respected and must be integrated in our constitutions and laws at the national and international level. We should actively protect biodiversity from the monocultural mass production and mass consumption that come with industrial economies. We need legislation that protects Nature and biodiversity, that acknowledges their intrinsic value.

We need to relearn to give greater importance to the well-being of the planet and the well-being of humanity, rather than privileging economic growth, production, consumption, profit, and money. These are means to an end. The end is the well-being of our planet and its biodiversity, which includes human communities.

We can create a new way of moving through the world. A new paradigm. By changing our motivations and intentions, everything changes. Whatever we do, we can do as a service to all living beings, as an act of universal love for the diversity of life. We can recreate a more harmonious and loving relationship with our planet. We can feel at one with Nature. We can change our materialistic, consumeristic, economic worldview into a holistic worldview by cultivating a love for diversity.

We have to create a new economy, a natural economy, an economy of love.

Nature is abundant and never wastes. The fruit that is not eaten returns to the soil and fertilizes it: a perfect system. We can learn everything we need to learn about diversity from Nature. Nature is our teacher. Nature is our mentor. All we need to do is attempt to understand her teachings.

If we want to create a new paradigm—a new economy—a civilization in which humans and Nature can live in harmony, then we have to start by creating a new kind of education rooted in the principle of diversity. As we learn science, mathematics, history, and geography at schools and universities, we also need to learn to love diversity of Nature and diversity of people. Learning to love diversity and to be compassionate is as fundamental to life as learning where we come from and where we're going. From an early age, we must celebrate biodiversity and cultural diversity of our precious planet Earth.

5

An Ecology of Love

Love is in the flower / you have to let it grow.

—JOHN LENNON

It was Arne Næss, a Norwegian philosopher, who made the distinction between Shallow Ecology and Deep Ecology. Shallow Ecology considers nature conservation important but only in that Nature is useful to humans. It's an anthropocentric world view. In this view, humans are the special and superior species. The natural world exists for one purpose and one purpose only: to serve human needs. According to Shallow Ecology, humans should take care of the environment—the animals, the oceans, the rivers, and the forests—so that we can benefit from Nature for a long time to come. Shallow Ecologists desire a sustainable future for humanity and view Nature as a "resource" for the economy.

For the advocates of Deep Ecology, Nature has intrinsic value. Nature is not a resource for the economy, but the source of life itself. Trees are good, not just because they give us oxygen, take in our carbon dioxide, or give us shade, fruit, and wood. Trees are good in and of themselves. Trees, like oceans and mountains, were here before humans came on the scene. How can we say that humans are superior to Nature and that Nature is here for humans? Deep Ecologists recognize not just human rights, but rights of Nature. As such, Deep Ecologists view Shallow Ecology as a kind of arrogant human imperialism, in which humans profess to be the rulers of the natural world.

Love Ecology says yes to all that Deep Ecology claims, and adds an extra dimension: it considers Nature to be sacred. It says life is sacred, and that humans need to cultivate a sense of gratitude toward Nature.

All religions have a tradition of reverence for Nature. For Christians, the Patron Saint of Ecology was Saint Francis of Assisi, who convinced the murderous wolf of Gubbio to live in peace with its victims. There's a new awareness among many religious groups who consider it their sacred duty to plant trees, take care of the land, and otherwise be compassionate in farming and livestock practices. Reverence for life is a religious impetus. It's a religious responsibility to be generous and to be kind to Nature. Having a sense of gratitude for all the gifts of life that we receive every day is a spiritual imperative. How can we disregard, disrespect, and destroy Nature if we believe that Nature is God's creation and God's gift?

Shallow Ecologists believe that Nature is inanimate. We humans have mind, intelligence, and consciousness. But from

Love Ecology's point of view, Nature also has mind, spirit, soul, and intelligence. The apple seed has memory: it knows exactly what to become. To be or not to be might have been a question for Shakespeare's Hamlet, but it is not a question for the apple seed. The seed of being is never confused. It knows its true nature. It knows who it is, what it is, and what it wants to be.

When I was a little boy, my mother would tell me to revere the trees.

"Why, mother?" I asked.

"The tree is our teacher, and it is the greatest teacher in the world," she replied. "Even greater than the Buddha."

"Mother, this can't be true," I objected. "There's no greater teacher than the Buddha. He was our greatest teacher."

"My son, where did the Buddha obtain enlightenment? It happened while he was sitting under a tree. Nowadays, we don't find enlightenment because we don't sit under trees. When the Buddha was sitting under the tree, he learned the principle of harmony in the Universe. The sun and the rain are in harmony with the tree. The tree is taking nourishment from the soil, and that soil is transformed into fruit. The fruit is giving nourishment to people, to the birds, and to the bees. All phenomena are interconnected and interdependent. We are all related. The Buddha learned all that from trees."

The moment we realize that we are all related, this planet becomes our home. The birds flying in the sky are our kith and kin. The deer and the rabbits in the forest are our siblings. Even tigers and elephants, snakes and earthworms are members of one Earthly family. Without the earthworm, there will be no food on our table. The earthworm works day and night, without a weekend, without a holiday, without any wages. Long live the earthworms, I say. Darwin developed his theory of evolution by studying earthworms, so let us be grateful to earthworms for the gift of understanding. The moment we have that sense of gratitude, we have an ecology of love.

In the perspective of Shallow Ecology, humans and Nature are separate. In the Love Ecology, humans and Nature are one. We are all made of earth, air, fire, water, and space. Everything in the Universe is in us. Without the sun or the moon, we cannot be. We are each a miniature Universe, a microcosm of the macrocosm. Within a Love Ecology, humans realize the expansive unity of life, and all our narrow, petty disconnections disappear. In an ecology of love, we are all members of one Earth community, one family. With that consciousness we are released from the burden of separateness. We shift from egocentrism to ecocentrism, transforming our entire worldview. It is here that we touch the mind of God.

In concluding his book *A Brief History of Time,* the scientist Stephen Hawking said that we would one day know the mind of God. With Love Ecology, we can know the mind of God in this very moment. God is not somewhere beyond the sky. God is everywhere in the cosmos. God means cosmic consciousness. We just need to expand our consciousness and know that each of us is a cosmos in miniature. All the cosmic forces are in us, and we are in the cosmos. Love Ecology enables us to feel at home and at ease on this beautiful planet and in this wonderful cosmos.

6

A Love Trinity

Keep from single vision and Newton's sleep.

—WILLIAM BLAKE

Radical Love is a vision of total transformation and a vision of holistic harmony. Existence is a multidimensional reality and not a single-dimensional view. We make our lives most perfect through a love of Nature: Soil; a love of oneself: Soul; and a love of others: Society. This is a love trinity for a new age.

In the Bhagavad Gita, Lord Krishna says to the warrior Arjuna that from the very beginning of life one exists in three dimensions: the natural, spiritual, and societal. The five elements are a gift to all life from the universe. As humans, we breathe air and drink water to support life. We grow food in soil to sustain ourselves. We use fire for cooking and warmth, and it is in space we live. The economy of the universe is a gift economy, based on reciprocity. It is not a theft economy, creating waste and pollution and inequity. It is our responsibility to ensure that the five elements are maintained in good order, kept clean, pure, and replenished on a regular basis. In the Vedic tradition, this act of replenishment is called *yagna*, which means love of Nature, or love of soil, as soil symbolizes all the natural elements.

From the day of our birth, we have been given a body, senses, intelligence, and a soul: the self, our whole being. As we are required to maintain the purity and integrity of the five external elements for our well-being, we are also required to remain constantly mindful of the purity, integrity, and health of our intimate elements: our mind, body, spirit, and intelligence. As we live our lives, we are bound to experience exhaustion, burnout, stress, and even despair. Therefore, it is our responsibility to find ways and means to replenish, recuperate, and nourish our souls, our own selves. Such self-care is not a selfish act; it is an imperative and a prerequisite for the care for others. This self-care is known as *tapas*, which means love of oneself, or soul love.

We are not born as isolated and disconnected individuals. We are members of our families, our neighborhoods, our communities, and our wider societies. As we have the gifts of food, water, air, and warmth from Nature, and the gifts of imagination, consciousness, memory, and intelligence from our souls, we also have many gifts from our human community. These gifts include culture, architecture, literature, philosophy, religion, arts, crafts, and many more. We have received these gifts from those who lived in the past, and we continue to receive them in the present. We are not here merely to consume the gifts of others; we are responsible to offer similar gifts in return. We are required to contribute our creativity, our talent, and our skill as free offerings to enrich the social order. Such giving back to our communities should be in recognition of the fact of mutuality and reciprocity. When this is done with a sense of selfless service it is known as *dana,* which means love for all people irrespective of their caste, class, religion, race, or nationality.

These three timeless principles of the Bhagavad Gita—yagna, tapas, dana—are as relevant today as they were when they were first formulated thousands of years ago. I have adapted and reformulated these principles for our age, a new trinity for our time: Soil, Soul, and Society.

Our society encourages specialization of thought, but it is important to remember that this trinity represents three aspects of a holistic vision. There are those who might be tempted to devote themselves entirely to conservation and the protection of Nature, while spiritual or metaphysical dimensions fail to enter their consciousness. Others might devote themselves wholeheartedly to a spiritual quest—the practice of meditation and yoga, the study of spiritual texts and living a life of self-upliftment—with little concern for the preservation of the natural world. Others still might devote their lives to the causes of social justice, human rights, and economic equality. For them, spiritual matters may seem like self-indulgence and the conservation of nature something too far removed from human experience.

We must drop all preconceived notions for a moment and look at the holistic perspective offered by the Bhagavad Gita, which says that everything is connected and related. We are all made of each other. Nature, spirit, and humanity are three dimensions of one reality. Even if we are focusing on one dimension of our earthly existence, we need to be aware of the subtle and hidden links between the outer and the inner, between the social and the spiritual, and between the natural and the industrial.

Those who are concerned with conservation of Nature need to remember that Nature is not just *out there.* Caring for humans is as much part of Nature conservation as caring for wildlife. Similarly, upholding the rights of Nature is as much part of human rights as working for social justice and economic development.

Nature and humans are not just physical entities. The earth and all living beings upon it, humans and other-than-humans, are living, complex organisms. We are embodiments of compassion, generosity, humility, and love. If we have a good social order and a clean environment but no joy, empathy, or love, then what would life be? We need a clean environment, a just social order, and a flourishing personal life in equal measure; we need spirituality and love in our hearts to be fulfilled. This is what Lord Krishna says to Arjuna: there is no fragmentation or disconnection between the natural, the spiritual, and the social. We are an integrated whole.

7

Soil

The soil is the great connector of lives,
the source and destination of all.

—WENDELL BERRY

Soil is the source of life on Earth. Everything here comes from the soil and returns to the soil. If we take care of the soil, the soil takes care of us and all our needs. The soil gives us food, trees, and water. The soil holds us and our dwellings on her back, yet she is so humble that she always remains under our feet.

Soil is also called "humus," from the same root as *human*— what a wonderful connection: human beings are literally soil beings. Humans need to be respectful of humus; they must practice *humility,* a word which also derives from the same root. As does *humidity.* Humility is related to humidity. Through humidity the soil is nourished, and through humility the soul is respected. These are meaningful words: *humus, human, humidity,* and *humility.*

An industrial civilization considers the soil inert and uses chemicals and fertilizers to give it life. This shows our ignorance—our lack of *humility*—and our failure to appreciate the living nature of the soil.

The time has come to celebrate the magic of Mother Earth.

The word *culture* is also related to soil. According to the Oxford English Dictionary, until the end of the eighteenth century, *culture* meant "a cultivated field or piece of land." In other words, the cultivation of the soil. From this we derive the term *agriculture.* Thus Nature and culture are united. One could not be cultured without cultivating the soil and nurturing Nature. In the nineteenth and twentieth centuries, *culture* became associated with cultivation of the soul and the imagination through music, poetry, painting, and dance. Those who cultivated the soil knew they were also cultivating the soul. Through folk dance, folk music, and folk paintings, the farmers nourished their souls while caring for the soil. Culture is the bridge between soil and soul, between humus and humans.

With the rise of modernity, industrialism, and urbanism, the concept of civilization emerged. *Civil* and *civility* mean "of, or pertaining to, the city." Those who lived in cities called themselves civilized citizens, and started to look down on peasants, rural folks, and farm laborers. For many, dirt became "dirty," and this shift of consciousness meant leaving a life on the land to live in the city. Those who cultivated the soil and derived their livelihood from agriculture were now thought to be "uncivilized."

The mission of modernity was, and still is, to bring people into cities, where they work in factories, shops, and offices, rather than on the land. Of course citizens still need food. So food is produced not by agriculture but by agribusiness and industrial-scale factory farms. Mass production of mono-crops using heavy machinery and robots has become the modern way of farming. It is no longer necessary for farmers to cultivate the soil or even to touch it. Their job is to mind the machines, drive massive combine harvesters and tractors, and let robots do the milking of cows, the slaughtering of pigs, and even the sowing and harvesting of crops.

The unintended consequence of this shift from culture to civilization has been that agriculture has become totally dependent on fossil fuels. We are facing the massive problem of carbon dioxide emissions in the atmosphere. Twenty to thirty percent of CO_2 emissions is related to industrial farming, and a similar amount is related to food transportation, refrigeration, and disposal of food waste.

Who would have thought that our progress, development, modernity—our civilization—would threaten our very existence? In addition to this external insecurity caused by climate change, "civilized" societies are suffering from internal insecurity as well. We are living in an age of anxiety. Lack of life fulfilment and lack of job satisfaction are causing disillusionment and even depression.

The underlying cause of this external and internal insecurity is our separation from and disconnection with the soil. Under the influence of civilization, modern societies have ceased to know that humans are related to humus. The imperative of our time is to cultivate love for soil. We are an integral part of soil. What we do to soil we do to ourselves. If we continue to poison the soil, we will face the consequences.

Change begins with putting our hands in the soil and expressing our love and gratitude to soil for being so generous and abundant in providing us with physical and spiritual nourishment. Celebration of the soil is a celebration of life. Soil is good. Soil is virtuous. Soil is beautiful. Soil is wise. By connecting with the soil, we connect with the whole of the cosmos.

8

Seeds

Whatever happens to seed affects the whole web of life.

—VANDANA SHIVA

A seed is a miracle.
A small apple seed is the home of a huge apple tree.
Look at this apple seed.
This small seed contains a tall tree.
From this little apple seed we get that mighty apple tree.
That tree has been there for the last fifty years.
That tree has given us thousands of apples.
Each apple has another six seeds.
From one single seed we can create a whole orchard of apple trees!
Seed is so powerful.
How can a tiny apple seed become a great apple tree?
Let us find the answer.
The seed has to let go of itself.

We have to plant the seed in good soil.
We will never see that seed again.
The soil will take care of the seed.
Without the soil the seed cannot become an apple tree.
After a few months the seed is born as a small seedling.
It is so tender.
It is a small and beautiful plant.
We have to have a lot of patience and trust.
We have to learn to wait and watch it grow.
We give some water to the seedling for nourishment.
Without water there can be no apple tree.
Thanks to soil and water the seedling becomes strong.
It forms trunk and branches.
This is pure magic.
On these branches lots of green leaves grow.
In the spring suddenly there are wonderful blossoms.
They are pink, white, and awesome.
The bees buzz around them and pollinate them.
Without the bees there can be no apples.
From these soft flowers baby apples are born.
The warm summer sun helps them ripen.
Without the sun there can be no apples.
Thanks to the sun, soil and water, apples starts to mature.
They become colorful and fragrant.
They become sweet and juicy.
They become apples.
Come the autumn, the apples are ready to nourish life.
The apple tree is very kind.
The apple tree has boundless love.

The apple tree gives apples to everyone, as a gift.
The apple tree never asks, "Have you got some money on you?"
"Whoever you are, have apples," the tree seems to say.
Rich or poor, young or old, black or white, "have apples."
The apple tree never discriminates against anyone.
This is boundless love from the tree.
The apple tree is nourished by the sun, soil, and water.
The apple tree in return nourishes humans,
animals, birds, and insects.
Apples are a gift from the universe.
We receive this gift with gratitude.
The apple tree knows the cycle of life.
We get tree from the seed.
We get seeds from the tree.
The apple tree is made of soil.
With its leaves the apple tree feeds the soil.
The apple seed has memory.
The apple seed remembers how to become an apple;
it never becomes a pear.
An apple tree is a work of art.
Artists paint the apple tree.
We take photos of apple trees laden with colorful fruit.
Poets write songs in praise of apple trees.
Scientist Isaac Newton saw an apple falling from a tree and
discovered gravity.
The Buddha sat under a tree and became enlightened.
The tree of life comes out of a humble seed.
Without the seed there is no tree.
Without the tree there is no seed.

Seed, sun, soil, water, and bees are in harmony with trees.
The seed is humble; it is happy to be in the soil under our feet.
Yet it produces thousands of apples for everyone.
A seed is a miracle.

9

Water

Rivers know this: there is no hurry;
we shall get there someday.

—A. A. MILNE

Situated on the banks of the river Dham, near the town of Wardha in Central India, my teacher Vinoba Bhave has his ashram. Once, as young man, I visited him there, and we were walking in the early morning along the river. It was the perfect time of day to enjoy the words of wisdom flowing like the purest water from the mouth of this great sage.

"Be like water, my friend."

"How should I be like water?" I asked.

"Flow like water. Even when it is in a lake, water keeps flowing. My favorite form of water is a river. Always on the move. Never fixed. Never stagnant. Never attached."

"How else should I be like water?" I asked.

"Live within your limits," said Vinoba. "A river flows within the limits of its two banks and it is free. You too can enjoy your freedom when you know your limits and practice restraint."

"What else can we learn from water?" I asked.

"Be as flexible as water," said Vinoba. "If you put water in a bottle it takes the shape of the bottle. If you put it in a glass it takes the shape of the glass. Water accommodates itself to its environment, yet it never loses its identity. You too can be true to your nature yet never conflict with your surroundings, your neighbors, your family, or your friends. Water has no enemies. Water is always there in the service of plants, animals, and humans quenching their thirst and nourishing all life. We humans too should always be in the service of others. That is what I have learned from water. Water lives to maintain the life of others."

"Are you saying that I should look at water as my teacher?" I asked.

"Yes, that is exactly what I am saying!" exclaimed Vinoba. "Water is so soft that you can drink it. You can put it on your eyes. You can swim in it. Yet water is also very powerful. Over time even jagged rocks under water become smooth. And over a longer period of time water turns rocks into sand. Never underestimate the impact of soft power! Even a great fire out of control is overcome by the power of water. Therefore, I say to you, my friend, be like water." We paused and were silent a moment beside the river. "Water is not a commodity," he said at last. "Water is more than a resource. Water is the source of life. Water is sacred. Wasting or polluting water is a sin against Nature. Love water."

I was born in the Thar Desert of Rajasthan, also known as the Great Indian Desert. It is the world's seventeenth largest desert and the biggest in India. It is 120,000 square miles, of which 60 percent is in Rajasthan. So I am a child of sandy, dry land. If we received six weeks of rain per year, we considered ourselves fortunate. Every drop of water falling on our rooftop was saved in our water tank, which we used for drinking, cooking, and bathing. Growing up, water was scarce and precious. I spoke of this to Vinoba that day as we stood by the river, thanking him, and assuring him that his talk about water resonated with me deeply.

Vinoba was reminded of a tale that has since become famous throughout India but which I was about to hear for the first time. As we made our way back along the river, Vinoba relayed the story of Mahatma Gandhi's visit to the stately home of the Nehru family, in the city of Allahabad. The house was known as Ananda Bhavan, the Palace of Joy. It was 1942, and Mr. Nehru was five years away from becoming the first Prime Minister of India.

Despite the house's relative luxury, there was no piped water. In the morning, Nehru himself brought a jug full of water and a wash basin for Gandhi. Nehru had a towel over his left arm and with his right hand he poured water into the basin while Gandhi washed his face and cleaned his teeth. As he poured the water, Nehru asked Gandhi about his plans to convince the majority of Indians to follow the path of nonviolence in the fight to end British rule in India. Gandhi explained that their example and wholehearted conviction would be the best way to convince others.

"Sorry, Bapu," interrupted Nehru, suddenly anxious. "Will you wait for a minute while I get some more water?"

"Have I finished all that water?" Gandhi asked, visibly perturbed. "I should have concentrated on my washing and should not have been carried away by all these big ideas at the same time. I should have finished my wash with one jug of water. I should have been more mindful."

"Bapu, don't worry about it. I know you come from Gujarat, a dry and desert land, where water is scarce. But here we have no shortage of water. Two great rivers meet here in our city of Allahabad, and there is even a third river, a mythical river, which keeps the water table high in our wells."

"Nehruji, you may have three rivers flowing through your city but that gives me no right to waste water. My share is one jug a day only."

Nehru noticed tears in Gandhi's eyes, which moved and surprised him. It was then he realized Gandhi was truly a man of self-restraint. He convinced Gandhi to allow him to bring half a jug of water, as an exception, so that he could complete his wash. When Nehru returned with the water, Gandhi resumed his bathing.

"I know you will think that I am being faddish," he said, "but I believe that there is enough in the world for everybody's need but not for anybody's greed, not to mention anybody's waste. Especially water, which is particularly precious; water is life itself. Abundance of it does not give us license to waste. We were just speaking about nonviolence; for me waste is violence."

We concluded our walk by the river Dham, and I thanked Vinoba for sharing his wisdom and tales with me. He motioned toward the river one last time. "Water is our teacher and the source of our lives. We need to learn to love and respect it, and use it with gratitude and humility."

10

An Ode to Mother Earth

December 1972
People say, "I want to go to heaven when I die." In reality, you go to heaven when you are born.

—JIM LOVELL, NASA ASTRONAUT

When I saw NASA's iconic image of the Earth, I instantly fell in love with that magnificent "blue marble." And through this incredible image, I fell in love all over again with the Earth herself. I wrote this ode to Mother Earth.

> I was looking at a precious blue pearl in the cosmic ocean.
>   A miracle in the cosmic mind.
> In that ecstatic moment I said to myself, this is Gaia, my living goddess.
> This is Mother Earth, my beloved mother, and the mother of all living beings.

This is our home, our only home, the home of humans,
animals, mountains, rivers, forests, oceans, and trillions
of life forms.

This is the self-sustaining, self-managing, and self-reliant
living Earth.

Mother Earth sustains herself and nurtures all her children
with food, water, air, and warmth.

She provides clothes, homes, energy, arts, crafts, and culture
to all without any discrimination or judgment.

Sometimes we humans take our benevolent Mother Earth
for granted.

Like naughty children we behave badly and act disrespectfully.

We pollute the water, poison the soil, and contaminate the
air.

We waste energy and disregard the limits of our mother's
capacities and threaten the life of our own mother.

We create conflicts and wars in the name of religion, political systems, nationalism, or some other superficial and
artificial boundaries.

Mother Earth has worked hard, over billions of years, to
evolve and create biodiversity, cultural diversity, and
truth diversity, but we humans turn delightful diversities into dreadful divisions and then fight over those
divisions and kill each other.

Through the image of the beautiful Blue Marble, our Earth
is reminding us that we should transcend these artificial
and superficial divisions and protect and conserve the
wonderful diversity of life and at the same time celebrate the unity of life.

After all we are members of one Earth family.

Mother Earth is certainly looking after us. Are we looking
after our Mother Earth?

Mother Earth loves us. Are we loving her in return?

I am certainly in love with this magnificent Blue Marble.

The Earth is the apple of my eye.

I will do everything in my power to look after our Mother
Earth.

Meditation on the Four Elements

Earth is a spiritual guide.

Earth is patient, forgiving, and generous.

Earth feeds all living beings without discrimination and without judgment.

May I learn to practice patience, forgiveness, and
generosity from the Earth.

May I be like Earth and be kind to all.

I salute the Earth.

Air is a spiritual guide.

Air is sustaining, invigorating, and energizing.

Air maintains life for all beings; a life of a saint
or a sinner, a human or an animal, a snake or a
spider, a mountain or a monkey.

May I learn from air to sustain, invigorate, and
energize all life without discrimination or
judgment.

I praise the air.

> Fire is warming, purifying, enabling, and
>   enlightening.
> Fire is a spiritual guide.
> Fire comes from the sun.
> Fire dispels the darkness.
> May I be the light for those who are lost in the
>   darkness and warm those who are suffering
>   from frozen heart, whoever they are.

I pay homage to the fire.

> Water is a spiritual guide.
> Water is softer than a flower and stronger than a
>   rock.
> Water quenches thirst and nourishes all creatures
>   of the Earth, irrespective of their being good
>   or bad, kind or cruel, poet or prisoner, poor or
>   rich.
> Water keeps flowing, overcoming all obstacles,
>   and purifying herself by flowing.
> May I be like water and quench the thirst of all,
>   deserving or undeserving.
> May I learn from water to be soft and strong at
>   the same time.

I bow to the water.

PART TWO

Radical Love Globally

Love recognizes no barriers.

—MAYA ANGELOU

11

An Ecological Worldview

We have forgotten how to be the good guests,
how to walk lightly on the earth as its other creatures do.

—BARBARA WARD

Ecology and economy are like siblings. Both words come from the Greek root *oikos,* which means "home" or "household." *Logos* means "knowledge," while *nomos* means "management." So we can think of ecology as "knowledge of the household" and economy as "management of the household." In the minds of Greek philosophers, *oikos* is a very inclusive term. It is where a family gathers in bedrooms, living rooms, and kitchens, but a nation is also *oikos,* and ultimately the entire planet is *oikos.* Amazing animals, fabulous forests, majestic mountains, awesome oceans, and of course imaginative and creative human beings are all members of this one planetary household.

If we were to meditate on the original and actual meaning of the word *economy,* we would soon realize that it is a subsidiary of ecology. Without ecology there can be no economy.

Endless production, consumption, and the pursuit of profit in the name of economic growth, progress, and development have become the most cherished goals of the modern world order. Nature, which is another name for *oikos,* is considered a resource for the economy. Natural resources, including people, have become means to an end—instruments to increase the profitability of businesses and corporations. We even call it "human resources."

According to an ecological worldview, production and consumption, as well as money and profit, should only ever be a means to an end. The end goal is the well-being of people, and the integrity of the planet. If production, consumption, and economic growth damage Nature and exploit people, then such economic activities must be stopped at once.

Production and consumption are necessary. However, from an ecological worldview, they must be pursued with restraint and in a manner that respects a natural equilibrium. In the economy of Nature there is no waste. It is therefore an ecological imperative that human production and consumption of goods and services do not produce waste. Waste is violence to the ecological integrity of our planet. Whatever we take from Nature must return to Nature. What cannot be reabsorbed should not be produced.

An industrial economy is a linear economy. We take natural material from the Earth, process it, use it, and then toss it. The consequence is that too much ends up in landfills, in oceans, and in the atmosphere. We need to replace this linear economy with a cyclical economy. All goods and products must be engineered in a way that guarantees their safe return to Nature, without waste.

In an economy of Nature, there is no pollution either. If we let ourselves be guided by the wisdom of an ecological consciousness, we too can avoid polluting the Earth. Pollution is a violation of the purity and beauty of our home. If we pollute the air, we still have to breathe it; if we pollute the water, we still have to drink it; and if we pollute the soil, we still have to eat the food it produces.

My mother used to teach me that whatever we produce and consume should have three characteristics. First, it should be beautiful. Beauty is nourishment for the soul. Our senses and spirits are nurtured by beauty, which ignites creativity and inspires the imagination. Second, what is beautiful should also be useful. There is no contradiction between beauty and utility. Form and function must be harmoniously combined. Third, what is beautiful and useful should also be durable. What we produce and make today should have a long life. Built-in obsolescence is violence against nature. This formula—beautiful, useful, and durable (BUD)—should inform the study of economics.

We can learn about the BUD formula by looking to Nature and studying what she produces. Trees are beautiful. They are lovely to look at, they have natural balance and proportions, but they also have great usefulness. They absorb carbon dioxide and provide oxygen. They offer shelter to birds, who nest among their branches, and they provide food for humans and animals alike. Finally, trees have long lives. An oak or a yew tree can stand for a thousand years.

With an ecological worldview we transform the attitude that views the natural world only in terms of its usefulness to humans. We recognize the unity of human beings with all other living beings. We recognize the intrinsic value of all life, human life as well as other-than-human life. As we uphold human rights, we also uphold the rights of Nature.

Universities around the world teach courses on economics. This means they should be teaching youth how to manage our Earthly household. I was once invited to the London School of Economics (LSE) to discuss an ecological worldview. Before my talk, I asked some of the professors if they offered courses that allowed students to study an ecological worldview. They told me they offered courses on Environmental Policy and Economics as well as Climate Change and Economics, but no course on an ecological worldview as such. I suggested that "environment" and "ecology" were not the same, and that climate change was a consequence of harmful economic growth, whereas the study of ecology would encourage knowledge, understanding, and experience of the entire ecosystem and how diverse forms of life relate to each other.

LSE has taught thousands of young leaders from around the world about the techniques and methods of economic management. The world economy is in their hands, and sadly it is not in good order. But LSE doesn't teach ecology. This means that they are not teaching what this Earthly household is. They are teaching students to manage something without teaching them what it is that they are going to manage! This is not only a problem at LSE. Universities in every country around the world teach economics without a focus on ecology. It is a problem of our entire educational system. We have forgotten the true meaning of "economy."

Much emphasis is devoted to the management of money. Economics has been reduced to the management of money and finance in the interest of a particular group of people, rather than in the interest of all members of our Earthly household. The integration of ecology with economy is essential. This is why I encouraged LSE to embrace an ecological worldview by becoming LSEE, the London School of Ecology and Economics, making a public and unequivocal statement that all study at the university would be underpinned by an understanding of our Earthly household and its proper management. By taking such a bold decision and becoming LSEE, other universities would be on notice that the teaching of economics is incomplete without the teaching of ecology. As it stands, by ignoring an ecological worldview, academic institutions around the globe remain part of the problem.

12

A Love Economy

*Money is like love; it kills slowly and
painfully the one who withholds it, and enlivens
the other who turns it on his or her fellow man.*

—KHALIL GIBRAN

Across the globe, people are obsessed with money. And apart from the leadership in one small country—Bhutan—every nation in the world is under the spell of economic growth. The growth paradigm has essentially taken the place of religion today. It is the one common factor that binds almost all of humanity. It is the faceless emperor who finally conquered the world. This march to ever higher economic growth is forcing a set of choices that, in the end, contrary to helping us solve the burning problems of our time, confront us with the greatest challenges humanity has ever known.

Consider the United States of America, which has long since been one of the richest and most developed nations in the world. And yet no amount of growth has helped to resolve problems of poverty, inequality, homelessness, and disease. Additionally, the United States has become steadily more violent over the years. Gun violence and mass shootings have shocked the world again and again. Substance abuse has run rampant. More and more people are addicted to opiates in America. There seems to be no end to the violence, depravity, and depression that plagues this wealthiest of nations.

If this is the state of a nation with so great an economy—a trailblazer of economic growth, with relatively vast amounts of land and natural resources—then what hope can there be for other countries?

The simple truth is that the pursuit of economic growth will not bring us an end to poverty. Economic growth is driven by numbers and by the processes of short-term maximization of private profit and long-term exploitation of people and Nature. Economic growth cannot eliminate poverty because a new class of poor will inevitably be created and then left behind. The smooth ride on the concretized road of economic growth is a total illusion and we must become free of it if we are to end long-term damage to the Earth and her people. Infinite economic growth on a finite planet is not attainable. A time must come when we say enough is enough.

Instead, we can and must seek a new paradigm that shifts our focus from economic growth to growth in well-being: a Love Economy, which can arise only when people connect back to the land, appreciating the joyful and loving relationship it can provide. Coupled with a revitalized arts and crafts movement that helps everyone earn a livelihood, we can eradicate many of the issues that plague societies on a global scale. Modern day conveniences will then be the icing on the cake. In today's society, the icing is being mistaken for the cake, and this kind of sugar rush spells doom for all.

The leaders of tomorrow will be those who take this message of a Love Economy, rooted in the land, arts, and crafts seriously today, building upon new ideas and seizing leadership opportunities for a new era that is marked not merely by economic growth but by growth in wisdom, fulfilment, and happiness.

This is the true measure of growth, redefined for a new generation. A Love Economy provides limitless opportunities for people to grow and thrive in meaningful activities, rather than the pursuit of mindless jobs and throwaway wares.

Oikonamia—management of the household—as understood in its true meaning can be a force for good. Nature's own economy has sustained the planet for millions of years, but modern economic growth as defined by humans has sapped our resilience and strengths in less than a few hundred years.

Nations obsessed with limitless growth are on a dangerous path, attempting to obtain the impossible. With hindsight of the past one hundred years, it is evident that mere economic growth will not keep our citizens well-fed, well-clothed, well-housed, and well-educated, not to mention providing their well-being and happiness.

It is time to reject the linear notion of economic growth that has brought us the burdens of consumerism and pollution, and that can ultimately only lead to the destruction of our planet. Economic growth has been achieved by polluting our oceans, burning our rainforests, eroding our soil, destroying our biodiversity, and repressing our people with cheap labor and poor work conditions. Do we want this kind of economic growth? The economy of Nature celebrates a cyclical or a circular model, in which everything supports everything else.

In contrast with the destructive nature of a linear economy, a circular economy is a system of sustainable and regenerative economics. We need to replace money-based economics with love-based economics. The Earth gives everything to all living beings as a gift. Thus, Nature's economy is a Love Economy. Money should be seen as a means of exchange and not as a measure of wealth. True wealth is measured by the health of our land, people, and imagination.

The economy of education is another example of a Love Economy. The majority of people called to teach do so because they want to serve children as they learn, grow, and mature. Similarly, the economy of medicine is a Love Economy. Nurses and doctors care for the sick because they are called to serve, heal, and care for those in need. The economy of arts and crafts is a love of economy, in which artists and artisans love their handiwork, music, dance, poetry, painting, pottery, and carpentry. If all production of goods and services were carried out with love, there would be more beauty and creativity, more imagination and enjoyment, more happiness and harmony.

In the paradigm of economic growth, production and consumption become the purpose of life. Nature becomes a mere resource for making money and maximizing profit. People become the instruments of operating the money machine. But in an economics of love, production and consumption are simply means to an end. The end goal is human well-being and the well-being of the planet. It is the urgent imperative of our time to shift from economic growth to growth in well-being, to shift from an economics of money to an economics of love.

13

Localism

At the touch of love everyone becomes a poet.

—PLATO

A time of crisis is a time of opportunity. In the context of rising right-wing populism, there is an occasion to think afresh about the meaning of globalization and nationalism. For example, Brexiteers want to bring power back to Britain and take back control. Similarly, right-wing Republicans want to put "America first" and "make America great again." These are merely slogans, of course, and we must remember that life is about more than slogans.

On the one hand, Brexitiers want to move away from the European Union; on the other, they want even more globalization. They want to trade with the world, with New Zealand and Australia, with Asia and Africa, and with the Americas. This will require a great deal of transportation of goods and services around the globe. How much more fossil fuel will we need to transport products and services from continent to continent? What will be the impact of this global trading on the environment? At what rate will it accelerate climate change? And who is going to benefit from these global transactions?

Only the global players, the multinational corporations, and big business houses stand to gain. The rich will get richer while the poor stay poor. Globalization will increase dependence upon cheap labor abroad, while increasing unemployment at home, pollution of the environment, and waste of natural resources. The marriage of narrow nationalism with commercially driven globalism will feed inequality, unsustainability, and unhappiness.

Now is the time for a new vision of localism, in which people truly take back control of their lives, their economies, their communities, and their cultures, while putting a stop to senseless abuse of the environment.

Love of localism is the empowerment of local economies, local cultures, and local distinctiveness. Under the banner of localism, creativity of ordinary people through arts and crafts is honored. Economy and commerce have a place in society, but they must be kept in check, and not allowed to dominate our lives. Life is about more than commerce and consumerism. It is about communities and cultures, about beauty and sustainability, about skills and vocations. And human beings are more than mere consumers: we are also creators.

Love of localism encourages self-reliance. People grow and eat healthy and nutritious food, build beautiful houses, manufacture items of everyday use, promote the arts and crafts, and use science and technology wisely. Ideally, around 60 percent of goods and services should be sourced locally, 25 percent nationally, and only 15 percent globally. When this rebalancing happens, we will have truly taken back control of our economies.

It's important to note that localism and internationalism are complementary. We need to think globally but act locally. We can call it "glocalism," which is far from xenophobia, or a superiority complex. Narrow nationalism is a product of small minds and big egos, glocalism represents big minds and small egos. Glocalists honor and respect all cultures, all nations, all races, and all faiths. Mutuality and reciprocity are the glocalists' mantras. We believe in the international exchange of ideas and arts, music and poetry, dance and drama, science and philosophy.

Mahatma Gandhi talked about the decentralization of the economy and politics. Decentralization requires localization. E. F. Schumacher said that small is beautiful, and recommended keeping the economy on a human scale rather than on a global scale. We need to revisit the wisdom of such thinkers and organize an economy that is socially just, environmentally sustainable, and spiritually fulfilling. This economy must be grounded in human imagination, human skills, human creativity, human autonomy, human spirit, and above all love. Local economies bring about personal and social well-being to all people, while the global economies are dedicated to the maximization of financial profits for the 1 percent at the expense of social cohesion, ecological integrity, and human imagination.

This is not a time for despair. This is not a time for pessimists. Pessimists cannot be activists. To be activists we have to be optimists. We have to have the courage of our convictions. We have to move forward with hope. As Václav Havel said: "Hope is not the conviction that something will turn out well but the certainty that something makes sense, regardless of how well it turns out."

The time for building local economies is now! As the American poet Clarissa Pinkola Estés reminds us, "When a great ship is in harbor and moored, it is safe, there can be no doubt. But that is not what great ships are built for." Great ships go out in the sea, face the storms, and sail through. We are capable of sailing through the storms of right-wing populism. It is now the time of the environmentalists, the decentralists, the localists, the artists, and the activists. Can we rise to the challenge? Can we begin to build a movement of localism from bottom up? A grassroots movement of self-reliance and an economy of love? Nature herself is our model. Nature is self-sustaining and decentralized. An economy of nature is a local economy, free of waste and pollution, free of haste and exploitation. We need to learn from Nature and develop the economy of place, then we too will be able to free our economy from waste and pollution and bring environmental justice and social justice together.

14

Cities

New ideas must use old buildings.

—JANE JACOBS

I was visiting a friend in his offices near Oxford Street in Central London, when, after a cup of tea, he asked if I wanted to see his garden. I was surprised by the idea of a garden in the middle of so many offices, supermarkets, and department stores, but I followed my friend as he guided us upstairs to the roof. To my utter delight, we came upon a gorgeous garden—a rooftop full of herbs, plants, flowers, and even beehives.

My friend handed me a pot of honey, explaining that it had been produced by him right there. "The bees pollinate the plants and give us sweet, delicious, healing honey," he said proudly. "All this in the middle of London, isn't it a miracle?" For me it was an inspiring experience, as I had never seen beehives and lush gardens on the top of a building in central London.

People think of Central London as a concrete jungle. That, in order to have such gardens, we have to leave the city center, or, better still, go to the countryside for such luxuries. But, if we put all the roofs of London together—houses, offices, schools, colleges, and hospitals—there are thousands of acres of unused space available to cultivate. Now multiply that by all the great cities of the world. Why not use all this empty roof space to grow salads and berries, and offer refuge to honeybees?

My friend understands the true meaning of the word *company,* which comprises the Latin words *com*—together—and *pane*—bread. It is only when people share bread together that they can truly become a company. So in addition to rooftop gardens, offices should have kitchens where people can enjoy freshly cooked meals together for their lunch.

♡

When I visit a place of business, I ask my hosts if they are a company. The answer is always an emphatic yes.

"Of course we are a company!"

"Then show me your kitchen," I urge with a smile.

"What do you mean? We are not a restaurant."

"But to be a company you have to share your bread together. If you have no kitchen and no bread is baked and shared then how can you be a company?"

I am always touched when my little speech about the origin of the word inspires people to respond favorably to the idea. They can see how, if they were to share meals together, there would be more companionship. There would be more camaraderie and conviviality in the business, and this would make them better, stronger.

♡

Not only is there a huge amount of empty roof space begging to be used for greening every city, there are acres and acres of wall spaces, which could be transformed into vertical gardens. In some cities, ecologically minded gardeners have successfully experimented with the growing of peas, beans, carrots, and flowers along the walls.

In sunny cities around the globe, walls of high-rise buildings are waiting to be transformed into vertical gardens. In addition to producing food and flowers, these hanging gardens would provide extra insulation and create natural air conditioning against the heat. And in all cities north or south, wall gardens and roof gardens would provide the important benefit of reducing huge amounts of carbon dioxide from the environment, which will help mitigate the effects of climate change. Furthermore, if from time to time we leave our desks and screens to tend to roses and rosemary, thyme and tomatoes, connecting with the soil, and disconnecting from our technology, we will be saner and healthier human beings.

Gardening is not only good for feeding our bellies, it is good for our bodies, spirits, and minds. It is therapeutic. For those spending long days seated at their desks, occasional work in the rooftop garden, turning the soil and taking care of the compost, would offer mobility and exercise without the cost a gym membership, or the need to run on a treadmill. Roof and wall gardens are more than novelties and visual delights, they are health imperatives for city dwellers.

Cities must not be seen as the impediment to sustainability. Nearly 50 percent of the world's population now lives in cities. These populations are not suddenly going to move in favor of a rural lifestyle. Instead, we need to transform our cities into places of sustainable living, and this is entirely feasible.

♡

Another step toward sustainable cities is the use of solar power. Solar panels can be incorporated among the gardens on all city rooftops. Rather than using arable land for solar panels, we can use the roofs of city buildings where solar panels can coexist alongside our green gardens. There is no necessity to exchange food-producing land with energy-producing solar panels. We must protect sunny fertile fields to produce food.

As we collect solar energy from city rooftops, we can also collect water. This water would be very useful to irrigate the roof gardens and vertical wall gardens. Clouds bring water to all rooftops free of charge and without the use of fossil fuels. Rainwater is a gracious and generous gift of Nature. We should cherish it, celebrate it, and harvest it continuously. With roof gardens, wall gardens, solar panels, and water harvesting, we can make our cities less dependent on faraway resources, and minimize obstacles toward making cities eco-friendly.

15

An Urban-Rural Continuum

Never doubt that a small group of thoughtful,
committed citizens can change the world;
indeed, it is the only thing that ever has.

—MARGARET MEAD

If we love our cities, then we have to make them livable and sustainable. We also need to keep them on a human scale. The ideal size of a city should be no more than two million people. A citizen in any city should be able to walk to reach a restaurant, a library, a theater, or a shop. Cities on such a human scale should be surrounded by thriving and vibrant countryside, full of farms, orchards, and villages. For a sustainable and regenerative future, we need a harmonious urban-rural balance.

In the context of the consumerist culture of Hong Kong, the idea of conservation may sound like a contradiction in terms. Hong Kong Island, despite being a major global financial center and home to multinationals, is also just one of over two hundred islands that make up the region known as Hong Kong. Only 25 percent of Hong Kong's administrative area is built up, and that's where eight million people live, while the remaining 75 percent of the land comprises hills, woods, grassland, fields, and farms. Out of four hundred square miles of territory, three hundred need conservation, caring, cultivating, and protecting from the never-ending appetite of industry and its developers.

These so-called developers see a pristine landscape of meadows and fields as areas waiting to be developed, but Hong Kong, like every major center, has its share of ecowarriors fighting to protect her, and I'm happy to count some among them as my personal friends. They are the defenders of the so-called undeveloped, and they are setting wonderful examples that highlight that there is another economy besides the economy of banks, businesses, and builders. That is the economy of Nature, which constantly reminds us that natural resources are not merely the means to profit, but rather that Nature is the nourishing source of all life.

Forty percent of the administrative area of Hong Kong is designated as Country Parks and Nature Reserves. Not many people know of this fact. Even though much of the primary rainforest was cleared by developers after World War II, when a tsunami of building mania consumed the region, there are still secondary rainforests that need saving and safeguarding.

One of the champions of this conservation movement is the Kadoorie Farm and Botanic Garden, headed by my friend Andrew McAulay and his team of two hundred staff who work with diligence and dedication to uphold ideals of simplicity, sustainability, and spirituality. Together, they manage three hundred and fifty acres of permaculture and silviculture. Additionally, they run an educational program for local schools and welcome visitors from all over the world. The Kadoorie Farm was established by Andrew's uncle in the 1950s with the intent of providing the opportunity for poor farmers to help themselves.

Andrew is more than a conservationist; he is a poet and a philosopher. He has chosen a life in service of the planet and its people. Through his work promoting, protecting, and enhancing biodiversity, environmental awareness, and food production, Andrew has demonstrated that even in an economic center like Hong Kong, people can set a good example of nurturing Nature and protecting the future.

"Sustainability is not complete without spirituality," says Andrew. "We are conservationists not only out of fear but out of love; we love Nature, we love animals, plants, birds, and insects. In fact, all life. We want people to visit Kadoorie Farm and see what we are doing in order to experience Nature and know the beauty, generosity, and abundance of life. When they see, smell, taste, and touch the enthralling and vibrant qualities of natural life, they encounter something magical, mysterious, and vital."

The farm has become a shining example of agroecology, permaculture, natural farming, and organic agriculture. The process of food production is carried out as an integral part of the conservation of flora and fauna.

"All of us need food. We cannot survive without it, but food producers and farmers are looked down on. They are given little respect. The work of Kadoorie Farm is, in part, to restore dignity to farmers," said Andrew.

And he is right. The values and priorities of the modern world have grown so distorted that it is no wonder the life of our planet is in such a dire state.

Kadoorie Farm is not only an agricultural center, it is also a center for education, where I had the pleasure of teaching a course titled "Reconnecting with our Roots: Spirit, Culture, and Nature." Courses are held at the Green Hub, a restored police station built in 1899 in the town of Tai Po. Kadoorie Farm, in collaboration with the government of Hong Kong, has carried out eco-renovations of this important historical site in order to showcase a vision of sustainable living, while, at the same time, respecting and protecting the environment.

Situated on a hill and surrounded by ancient woodland, the Green Hub is an oasis of peace, tranquility, and serenity. People from all over Hong Kong come to see this imaginatively and pleasingly restored old police station, and to enjoy wholesome, organic, and delicious food in the Eat Well Canteen. The guiding principles of this eatery are to encourage people to learn to cook seasonal and locally sourced healthy foods, to eliminate waste, and to move away from meat consumption. These principles may seem commonplace to many these days, but in the context of the presiding food culture of Hong Kong, they represent a revolutionary concept.

Eat Well Canteen is not alone in its mission. Situated in the heart of Hong Kong Island, there is another eatery that upholds similar ideals. It is a vegetarian restaurant called MANA!, founded by Bobsy Gaia, who has pioneered the plant-based fast-casual market in Hong Kong since 2012. Despite his constant commitment and determination, Bobsy admitted that running an eco-friendly business in Hong Kong is no easy task.

"People in Hong Kong are busy," said Bobsy. "I want to offer them fast-slow food. I want to prove that you can have high quality food with fresh ingredients and zero waste; we now make compost with all our food scraps. In fact, two tons of them per month. These scraps are sent to organic farms where they become food for the soil. Food waste is a crime against Nature! Our motto is 'Eat Like It Matters.'"

Listening to Bobsy speak during a meal we shared at his wonderful restaurant, I reflected on the irony of a modern world in which hungry people are lining up for food while forty percent of food is thrown away from households, restaurants, and supermarkets in so-called developed countries that remain appallingly inefficient when it comes to food.

"The words *Hong Kong* mean 'fragrant harbor,'" explained Bobsy. "Once upon a time, people used to export timber, like sandalwood, that gave a sweet smell from the Hong Kong harbor. Thus the island got its name. Although that aromatic wood is no longer exported, the scent of our food together with sweet smelling flora are still here, and they need protecting."

The activities of Andrew and Bobsy are two beautiful examples of work rooted in love of nature, love of people, and love of Earth. For them, love is an integral part of a planetary consciousness. Each in its own way, Kadoorie Farm and MANA! remind us of the harmony that is not only possible but essential between the urban and the rural. Furthermore, they provide inspiration and example.

16

Bhutan

The purpose of our life is to be happy, and the sources of happiness are contentment, compassion, and love.

—HIS HOLINESS THE FOURTEENTH DALAI LAMA

When the fourth dragon king of Bhutan, Jigme Singue Wangchuck, was asked during a visit to New York in 1972 about the GNP of his country, he told the journalist he didn't know, then went on to say that, for him, the GNH—Gross National Happiness—was more important.

This spontaneous and inspired answer caught the imagination of the world and made headlines. Ever since, social activists, environmentalists, and economists around the world have been talking about GNH. Even several governments are beginning to measure happiness and well-being in addition to GNP and GDP. In 2011, the United Nations General Assembly passed a resolution making GNH an integral part of the development ideals. People are waking up to a new vision, which shifts the focus from economic growth to growth in well-being and happiness.

In 2014, Schumacher College and the GNH Centre in Bhutan launched a yearlong joint program on Right Livelihood, exploring the principles, economics, and practical applications of GNH. The course took place partly in the UK and partly in Bhutan. I was invited to teach on that course. My wife, June, and I traveled to Bhutan in March 2015, from Delhi to Paro via Kathmandu. Flying over the high Himalayan mountains and witnessing peak after peak of snow-covered wilderness was breathtaking.

Paro is the one and only international airport in Bhutan, and unlike other airports it is uniquely designed with traditional Bhutanese architecture. We were met by our friend and former Schumacher college student Gabby Franco, who had been volunteering at the GNH center for the past year and a half. After a one-hour drive we arrived in Bhutan's capital, Thimphu, and settled into our hotel, which also exemplified traditional Bhutanese architecture.

Again and again, we were impressed with how houses, hotels, shops, and office buildings were all designed in this distinctive style, and even adorned with local characteristics. No matter where we went, we felt a continued sense of having arrived—a sense of place.

In most modern cities this is not the case. Monotonous high-rise office blocks or housing estates are found in all corners of the globe. Whether in New Delhi or New York, one finds oneself in the same kind of concrete jungle of high-rise buildings. So being surrounded by simple, tasteful, and colorful architecture specific to Bhutan was a breath of fresh air.

Bhutan's former Prime Minister Jigme Thinley is a champion of GNH. During my stay, he held a luncheon at his home to discuss the GNH model of development. Situated on a hill overlooking the Thimphu Valley, Jigme Thinley's beautiful home was small and simple. He was a gracious, humble, and hospitable host. In addition to my wife and me, the now former Minister of Education Thakur Powdyel, and founding member of the Centre for Gross National Happiness, Saamdu Chetri, were in attendance. As we sat together, enjoying a delicious vegetarian meal, I was reminded of the power of such gatherings, simply being in each other's company, to do good in the world.

According to Jigme Thinley, the four basic principles of Gross National Happiness in Bhutan are as follows:

1. All development should be underpinned by the ideals of environmental sustainability and economic equality.

2. The conservation of biodiversity and natural habitat should be at the core of all human activities.

3. In the name of progress and modernity, the country must not destroy its traditional Bhutanese culture and Buddhist values.

4. Good, clean governance should be at the heart of politics.

These are wonderful aspirations, of course, but Jigme Thinley spoke of being a small country sandwiched between two behemoth ones obsessed with economic growth: China to the north and India to the south. "To be happy, we must be friends with both," he said, acknowledging the enormous pressure on Bhutan to embrace modernity and materialism. Moreover, with the spread of the internet and advertising, young Bhutanese want to modernize. They do not want to be deprived of access to television and digital culture. This small country faces a big dilemma: how can it conserve the old culture and exist in the twenty-first century at the same time? This was a central question explored and addressed throughout the course on Right Livelihood as well. "We need to remember and heed the teachings of the Buddha and the Dalai Lama," said Thinley. "These teachings always remind us that it is more important to be joyful than successful."

During our lunch and throughout the course, the conversation often boiled down to money, and the difference between employment and livelihood. We do a job because we are paid to do it. We are under the orders of an employer. If we must abide by the rules of a corporation or company, there is little chance to use our own initiative, imagination, or creativity. In this regard, an employee is mostly a cog in the machine of a bureaucracy.

Livelihood, however, is a confluence of profession and vocation. With right livelihood we love what we do and do what we love. Our proper livelihood emerges out of an inner calling. The exchange of money is merely a means to an end. In livelihood, the work itself has intrinsic value. There is a sense of contentment, fulfillment, and satisfaction in work. Livelihood is rooted in imagination, creativity, improvisation, and meaning. Whatever the occupation one chooses, whether a cook or a gardener, a potter or a painter, a designer or a dancer, one is first and foremost a maker, a creator, a poet. The word *poetry* comes from *poesis,* a Greek term for "making." As in *auto poesis,* or self-making. Everything we produce, compose, or create with our own imagination and initiative is poetry. All work should be poetry.

After lunch, Jigme Thinley brought us to see his large and resplendent garden, full of flowers, fruit trees, herbs, and vegetables. I was delighted to see a politician so proud of his garden, and told him so. "In politics I use my head," he said, "but here in the garden I can nourish my heart, use my hands, and keep myself fit!"

In 1973, E. F. Schumacher wrote an essay called "Economics in a Buddhist Country." This was the first time a Western economist chose to put those two words—*Buddhist* and *economics*—together. When asked what Buddhism had to do with economics, Schumacher replied, "Economics without Buddhist or ethical values is like flowers without fragrance or words without meaning. Right livelihood puts ethics and work together." In other words, GNH promotes livelihood rather than employment.

Only through right livelihood is one able to find contentment, compassion, and love as the true sources of happiness.

Through a combination of enlightened leadership, Buddhist values, and the aims of GNH, Bhutan is trying to choose a way of livelihood over an economy of employment.

The Dalai Lama says that you don't have to be a Buddhist to practice compassion and love, you just have to be compassionate and loving. In any case, Buddhism is not a religion; it is a way of life, of practicing compassion and love to find happiness. True happiness doesn't come through political power and position, or through money and material possessions. True happiness comes from love.

Bhutan is one of the smallest countries in the world, tucked away in the high Himalayas, where it might seem easy to escape from many of the traumas of our times. The truth is, however, that being such an ecological, spiritual nation in the modern world has never been more challenging. Yet we must remember that the modern industrial world was built by humans, so it can be managed and transformed by humans.

17

Ecological Civilization

Being deeply loved by someone gives you strength,
while loving someone deeply gives you courage.

—LAO TZU

China's history in recent years is one of great change. The Communist Revolution, the Cultural Revolution, the Industrial Revolution, and the Consumer Revolution all burst into China at breakneck speed. In recent years, China has experienced unprecedented growth and development, resulting in grave problems of air, water, and soil pollution. Such rapid industrialization has also led to mass migrations from the countryside to newly built urban centers.

In response to the devastation and degradation of China's long-beloved, precious natural environment, many citizens began looking for a long-term solution. Chinese religion, culture, art, poetry, and lifestyle have long been rooted in the idea of living harmoniously with nature. And yet, even such a longstanding, deeply enjoyed history was no match for the psychological and environmental crisis of rapid development. But out of this crisis, an opportunity presented itself for the Chinese to reexamine their modus operandi. In 2007, a new dream and promise of an ecological civilization emerged on the horizon. The idea was enshrined in the Communist Party's constitution, and as a first step the Ecological Civilization Association was established in Beijing, with several branches in regions and provinces throughout China. Soon, in each department of government a special unit was established to promote the vision and practice of an ecological civilization.

The prevailing sentiment was that the generation currently at the helm in China was interminably wedded to the pursuit of economic growth. Their minds and behaviors had been so conditioned by—and committed to—the paradigm of industrial civilization that the only hope for an ecological civilization was to prepare the next generation before their induction into the same paradigm.

The younger generation needed to be informed and educated in a new paradigm of conservation, sustainability, and ecology. Therefore, the Ministry of Education in China instituted many programs and courses to introduce the ideals and methods of an ecological civilization in several universities.

I wanted to know if this push for an ecological civilization was a genuine commitment to ecological values in everyday life or merely a collection of slogans and platitudes. I had no doubt that there was an interest in conservation on an intellectual and academic level, but I was curious to see evidence of its practical applications ten years after the Ecological Civilization Association's inception.

In 2018 I got my chance when I was invited to be a guest of the University of Agriculture and Forestry in the town of Fuzhou. The question at the heart of our deliberations was clear: How can we reconcile an ecological civilization with economic prosperity? As I contemplated the inherent challenges of this universal problem, I began to consider the trinity of Soil, Soul, and Society in the context of Chinese culture.

The three most culturally influential figures in Chinese history are Lao Tzu, Buddha, and Confucius. Together, they lay the foundations of an ecological civilization. We can formulate their teachings in the trinity of Soil, Soul, and Society, respectively. Lao Tzu was a natural philosopher, telling us "the people are ruled by the Earth, and the Earth is a sacred vessel." He also said, "Nature never makes an aesthetic mistake, and it is this perfection which allows us to rest in awe." His wisdom was rooted in Nature, and I see him as representing the voice of the soil.

The Buddha represents our absolute and unassailable unity with the spirit, what I call Soul. From a Buddhist perspective, ecology is not simply an external matter of organization, but should be built on the foundation of love and compassion. The Buddha said, "radiate boundless love toward the entire world; above, below, and across, unhindered, without ill will, and without enmity. Love without measure; love unconditionally and absolutely."

Confucius asks us to take total responsibility for ourselves, and to live in perfect harmony with all human beings. He represents Society. Human well-being on a mass scale—Society—along with the well-being of the planet—Soil—and the individual spirit—Soul—together constitute the whole of an ecological civilization.

The ideal of an ecological civilization is very much in line with the New Rural Reconstruction Movement initiated by Professor Wen Tiejun. This movement is active in reconnecting the Chinese economy with ecology through appropriate land uses, agroecology, rural crafts, and artisanal foods. In our deliberations, Professor Wen reminded us of President Xi Jinping's dictum: "China must maintain a right relationship between people and Nature. This self-evident truth is often overlooked because in the past few decades our country has been under the pressure of economic growth at all costs."

I asked Professor Wen if there wasn't a contradiction between President Xi Jinping's announcements and the Chinese pursuit of continuous economic growth.

"Yes, there is an apparent contradiction," Professor Wen replied, "but things cannot be changed overnight. Also, not everybody in the Chinese government is in total agreement with the ideals of an ecological civilization. China was facing grave poverty, so the government's first task was to bring millions of people out of poverty. That has been achieved. Now we can begin to change our direction. The president is a philosopher as well as a politician. He has said, 'There is only one Earth in the universe and humankind only has one homeland. Our green mountains and our clean rivers are as good as, if not better than, mountains of gold and streams of silver.' We in China want a symbiotic relationship between ecology and economy. The goal of an ecological civilization is better than the goal of sustainable development. Chinese civilization is an ancient civilization. It has been around for five thousand years. We must make sure that it lasts at least another five thousand years and more."

I also had the pleasure of meeting Mr. Wang, a spokes-person and leading light of the Chinese Ecological Civilization Research and Promotion Association in Beijing. "Ultimately our goal is to keep China beautiful," said Wang. "President Xi has also made this public claim. He said, 'any harm we inflict on Nature will eventually return to haunt us. Therefore, China must be the torchbearer in the global endeavor to address the challenge of global warming and put ecology in the driving seat on the train of economics.' It will be utter foolishness to take pure air, clean water, pristine soil, and blue sky for granted. If we pollute the air, infect the water, poison the soil, and fill the sky with greenhouse gases, we will be behaving like a fool who is cutting the branch on which he is sitting. Our ideal is that all nations must come together and embrace the concept of an ecological civilization."

I was moved by his words but felt compelled to point out that keeping air, water, and soil clean requires more than a policy decision. "We need to love air, water, and soil," I said. "We protect things we love! These resources are more than utilities; they are life itself. Love of life is the highest form of love, and only a civilization built on love will endure."

One can find faults and shortcomings in any country, but we must also look for signs of green shoots. The idea of an ecological civilization is an admirable green shoot in the land of China that can serve as a global source of inspiration.

18

Peace

We are asleep until we fall in love.

—LEO TOLSTOY

War and Peace by Leo Tolstoy is a story of love and betrayal, joy and sorrow, extravagance and deprivation. But above all it is an unambiguous articulation of the futility of war and the paramount importance of love as a prerequisite for peace.

After experiencing the despairing carnage of the battle-field, Prince Andrei says to Pierre Bezukhov: "War is the vilest thing in the world. Men come together to kill each other; they slaughter and maim tens of thousands and then they say their prayers of thanksgiving for having slaughtered so many people. How does God look down and listen to them?"

How indeed? If only the presidents and prime ministers of the world were required to meditate on this question before they acquired a public office. To accept the truth of truths, that war is hell and all wars end in unmitigated disaster, we need to courageously renounce war as a means of solving the world's political problems. This is Tolstoy's imparted wisdom; this is his gift to us in *War and Peace*.

Of course all warring parties claim to have higher ideals on their side. They claim to be fighting for their religion, or for democracy, or for national security, or to uproot the menace of terrorism. But religion, democracy, and security are the greatest casualties of war. And ordinary, innocent civilians—men, women, and children—are terrorized, while their homes, schools, shops, hospitals, mosques, and churches are destroyed. Because of wars, many countries experience a deluge of refugees. Millions of people are made destitute, forced to flee their homelands, and seek shelter in other lands, all for the ego and pride of those promoting wars that boil down to narrow self-interest, geopolitical ambition, and obsession with power. Yet it seems that few governments want to have refugees coming to their country. Providing food, jobs, accommodation, education, and medicine—not to mention a sense of community—for millions of people in a short time is not an easy or enviable task.

Wars create refugees. If governments don't want to have refugees, then they should not go to war. Whoever goes to war should be prepared to receive as many refugees as there will be. Waging a war and then barring entrance to refugees is a dereliction of duty. The same is true when dealing with a civil war. Countries not involved in the conflict still have an international humanitarian responsibility to support, sustain, and accept people who are fleeing their country because of war. And if a nation's military action causes civilians to flee, then it has an even greater obligation to accept refugees and support them until the conflict ends and refugees are able to safely return home. Nations involved in such wars have a further obligation to rebuild the homes, hospitals, schools, shops, and cities that have been destroyed so that refugees have a home to return to.

Politicians need to ask themselves why they choose war when there are no problems or disputes that ultimately cannot be resolved by diplomacy, negotiation, compromise, generosity, and mutual understanding. The whole of humanity has a shared common interest to live in peace and harmony together despite differences and diversities. Therefore, the wounds of all disputes, disagreements, and divisions can and should be healed by rising above narrow self-interest and embracing the interest of common humanity. As Mahatma Gandhi said: "There is no way to peace. Peace is the way."

The path of peace is paved by the principles of love and nonviolence. But governments need to recognize the falsity of claiming "our violence is good and righteous" but "their violence is bad and unjustified." Nonviolence and love are universal principles. We have to be prepared to minimize all forms of violence, and discard large-scale and organized violence. Politicians, like doctors, need to take the Hippocratic Oath to "Do No Harm" and follow that golden rule: One should treat others as one would like others to treat oneself.

♡

Violence begets violence. And love begets love. If you want to establish peace, democracy, and freedom, then that should be achieved through nonviolent means alone. Noble ends must be pursued by noble means. No matter how long it takes, we must have enough patience to restrain from violent responses, whether in the face of domestic violence, class wars, civil wars, or international wars. All wars are a failure of human ingenuity, negotiating skills, diplomacy, and imagination.

In modern warfare, it is impossible to avoid civilian casualties and collateral damage to schools, shops, hospitals, and homes. As wars turn innocent citizens into refugees, forcing them to flee from their homes and from their country, they are all ostensibly illegal. As the legally binding Geneva Convention states, "noncombatant civilians must not be inflicted with death and destruction."

Martin Luther King Jr. said, "An eye for an eye makes the whole world blind." We cannot put out a fire by adding more fuel to it. Jesus said it, the Buddha said it, Muhammad said it. Pope Francis says it. The Dalai Lama says it. Why do political and military leaders continue to disregard this practical wisdom from a long line of enlightened human beings? We have seen the enormous suffering of civilians and military personnel during small and great wars. We have evidence that wars don't work. You kill one dictator and another appears and takes his place with greater vehemence. You kill one terrorist but ten more are radicalized. The history of humanity is littered with failed wars and futile conflicts. The time has come to realize that wars are barbaric and uncivilized. They are counterproductive. Let the Security Council and the UN General Assembly pass the resolution to abolish war and establish a strong world council of negotiators to resolve conflicts wherever and whenever they arise.

Let us teach every child in every home and every school about cultivating love and peace for all in their hearts. If we do not nurture the seeds of violence in the hearts of human beings, they will dry out and die away. Let us, instead, nurture the seeds of love, peace, and nonviolence in every young human heart.

My own experience is that ordinary people around the world are kind, loving, peaceful, and generous. For more than two years, at the height of the Cold War, I walked around the world for peace, completely penniless and unarmed. During my eight-thousand-mile journey, I found no evidence of innate hatred in the hearts of humans. In fact, I was more often overwhelmed by the immense love and generosity of the so-called strangers I encountered.

19

Protest, Protect, and Build

We do not know enough to be pessimistic.

—HAZEL HENDERSON

Millions of people around the world are engaged in actions for change. For want of a better name, I refer to this collection of actions as the holistic environmental movement. "Holistic" to indicate that this is a global movement, committed to enhancing and safeguarding the integrity of the natural environment, the social environment, and the spiritual environment.

If the ecosystem is not in good health, there can be no social well-being, as it is not possible to have healthy people on a sick planet. Similarly, without social justice there can be no ecological justice, because if large numbers of people are oppressed and struggling for survival, they will not have the capacity, energy, or opportunity to be mindful of planetary well-being. And without spiritual values, such as love of people and love of our planet, underpinning and informing our worldview, ecological sustainability and social solidarity will remain superficial, only ever skin deep.

Those committed to a holistic environmental movement must act at three levels simultaneously: we Protest, we Protect, and we Build.

Protest

First, we Protest. We stand up against the unjust order, and against the forces that destroy the fragile ecological network and social systems.

All great movements of the past and present have used the way of protest to highlight the unsustainable exploitation of the natural world and the unjust subjugation of vulnerable people. Such subjugation is practiced to this day, under the guises of class, caste, race, religion, economic mobility, and so on. The actions of Extinction Rebellion and the school strikes of Greta Thunberg and thousands of other young people around the world are two recent examples of eco-activism using the way of the protest. Similarly, worldwide demonstrations organized by the Black Lives Matter movement are further examples of protest as social activism.

Protest movements, to be inclusive of all ordinary citizens, must be carried out nonviolently and peacefully. History shows that through nonviolent activism and passive resistance great changes have been and can be accomplished. The movements led by Mahatma Gandhi for India's independence and by Martin Luther King Jr. for racial harmony in the United States are two shining examples of nonviolent resistance, which apply the method of protest against unjust social orders.

Protect

To protest alone is not enough. We also need to protect the existing cultures and systems that are good, decentralized, regenerative, and sustainable, such as indigenous cultures, local economies, and human-scale organic farms. We need to protect biodiversity and cultural diversity. We need to protect beauty and the integrity of Nature.

In the name of progress and development, tried and tested social traditions and practices are constantly being destroyed. Indigenous communities are treated as backward, even savage, and forced to adopt the ways of so-called civilization. In this speedy urbanization, large numbers of thriving villages and rural communities are being devastated. In the process of rapid industrialization and mechanization, arts, crafts, and cottage industries are being eliminated. Self-sustaining small farmers, who still produce 60 to 70 percent of the world's food, are increasingly marginalized and their livelihoods are threatened. In pursuit of rapid globalization, local economies are stripped of power and agency. Of course we must protest against these trends and against energy-intensive production, wasteful consumption, and limitless carbon emissions, all of which are causing global warming. But we do more than protest: we work to ensure that these coherent communities and ancient cultures are respected, cherished, and protected.

Build

This stride toward protection of existing, durable cultures is also not quite enough. We must also build decentralized local economies, sustainable small-scale businesses, and regenerative farming projects, such as agroecology and permaculture. We also need to build new educational institutions and learning programs to teach the young and the old how to live well without damaging the integrity of our precious Earth, and without undermining the well-being of all life, human as well as other-than-human. We need to build community-owned energy systems derived from wind, water, and sun. In doing so, we are building new and resilient communities of people who are committed to a way of life rooted in solidarity, cooperation, and mutual aid. Successful examples will go on to inspire and persuade the unconvinced to engage in constructive activities, growing the movement and leading to an even more resilient and regenerative culture.

We protest, we protect, and we build, all with love!

♡

This trinity of Protest, Protect, and Build is not limited to external transformation only. To complement external transformation, we need internal transformation that nourishes the spiritual environment. To protest successfully against materialism, consumerism, greed, and lust for power and money, we need to embrace nonmaterialistic values. And to protect community cohesion and social harmony, we need to cultivate altruism and go beyond the egotistical chase for name, fame, recognition, status, and position.

By committing to a holistic environmental movement in which we Protest, Protect, and Build, one can't help but experience a simultaneous and equally essential evolution of spirit. This inner transformation means a change of heart, a change of attitude, a change of value and philosophy—a change of worldview, and ultimately a change of consciousness. External transformation goes hand in hand with internal transformation. They are two sides of the same coin!

Our actions need to be rooted in a deep recognition of the unity and dignity of life, and in a profound conviction that all life is sacred. By embracing a sense of the sacred we cultivate compassion and love for all life. We cultivate frugality, simplicity, moderation, and restraint. We become the embodiment of change while demanding external systems to change. Personal transformation and political transformation become a mutually supportive process, like walking on two legs.

The holistic environmental movement (HEM) goes beyond the dualistic trap of capitalism and socialism, both of which are anthropocentric, whereas the HEM is biocentric. Capitalism puts financial capital and the profit motive at the center of all human activity. In capitalism, people become instruments of profit, and Nature becomes a resource for the economy. Socialism, as the word implies, puts social interest above the interest of the natural environment. Historically, socialism has turned out to involve large-scale centralized and industrialized state capitalism. Democratic socialism is of course better than capitalism, but the word *socialism* remains anthropocentric. Environmentalists advocate social solidarity and social justice, but they do not, by definition, adhere to one particular political philosophy. Moreover, social justice and Earth jurisprudence are integral parts of each other.

HEM promotes local, decentralized, human-scale, pluralist, and bottom-up economics and politics through participatory democracy. Environmentalists put quality of life above quantity of production and consumption. They focus on the growth of the well-being of people and the planet rather than on economic growth. Within the view of Deep Ecology, economies and politics should serve the interest of Mother Earth as much as the interest of human beings. The rights of Mother Earth are as fundamental as human rights. There is no contradiction between the two.

We may never accomplish a perfect state of natural harmony, social solidarity, or personal enlightenment, but we keep striving toward such a balanced way of being. Transformation is a lifelong journey and not a destination. Transformation is a process and not a product. Transformation is continuous, active evolution; it is not a static state.

20

Action

Love is the way
messengers from the mystery
tell us things.
Love is the mother.
We are her children.
She shines inside us,
visible–invisible, as we trust
or lose trust,
or feel it start to grow again.

—RUMI

Throughout the world, social and environmental activists dedicate themselves to essential causes, fighting for justice and for our planet. And yet, despite years of campaigning, it can often feel like government and industry do not listen— like nothing is being done. Naturally, this leads to anxiety, disappointment, and even despondency. I once received a letter from a dear friend, an artist and eco-activist dedicated to the fight against the use of plastics. Like so many of his fellow activists, he had reached a seemingly hopeless degree of frustration, exhaustion, and burnout. What follows is his letter to me, as well as my response to him and any who find themselves in a similar state of disillusionment.

Dear Satish,

I have been very despondent lately because of the world's helplessness to resolve any of the crucial environmental issues we are facing. People are clamoring for change but political leaders are only interested in keeping power to themselves. As Jimi Hendrix so wisely said: "When the power of love overcomes the love of power, the world will know peace." That our world could be in such great danger in my lifetime feels like a huge failing, and it makes me feel guilty and helpless.

All the work we have done raising the awareness of single-use plastic has only moved the UK government to bring in a small tax on virgin plastic … but not until 2025! We are riding a huge populist-nationalist revival when countries should be uniting together not fighting. How else can laws to protect the environment be brought in and adhered to if one country holds an advantage over another?! Competition has to be replaced by cooperation.

Even the Chinese, who claimed to be committed to becoming the world's first ecological civilization, cannot resist responding to their slower economic growth by encouraging their more polluting factories to ramp up production. Apparently, the air quality in Beijing is the worst it has ever been as a result! Our greed will be our downfall…maybe it will be no bad thing if the human species is severely incapacitated from climate change!

But for those of us who have children and grandchildren it is a hard pill to swallow. I've even heard people with no offspring glad that they have not procreated because of the kind of world they are bequeathing. My own children are the first generation to be fearful for the future. Who can blame them?

I know that you have a much more optimistic view than this and I admire you for that, as well as your faith in humankind to transform itself. At the moment I cannot see from where it can emerge. The only pragmatic group that is really committed to stopping the British government and business on their brutal path is Extinction Rebellion. It is a noble commitment to sacrifice liberty for the environment. If I were in the UK, I too would be blocking roads! They call them the new suffragettes— they might succeed. Sadly, I think the only way radical action will happen is when the first serious environmental disaster occurs. People are beginning to be fearful of living by the sea, since there is talk of future danger from rising seas and storms.

Please give me some of your optimism, I need it!

With all my love,

James

Dear James,

I completely understand your doubts, despondency, and frustration about the state of the world, and the helplessness around the inability and unwillingness of governments to resolve the ecological issues of our time. The problem of plastic, about which you are so justifiably concerned, has been building up over a long period of time. Turning it around will take time, though I hope a much shorter time than it has been poisoning our planet. You are right to be concerned. The problem of plastic pollution, excessive emissions of carbon dioxide into the atmosphere, and the decrease in biodiversity are urgent issues that have created a situation of planetary emergency.

That said, when we are facing an emergency, I believe we need to act with great patience. As an example, if there is fire in a theater, we must vacate in an orderly manner, otherwise a stampede could cause more casualties.

Nevertheless, we must act and act with love, dedication, commitment, and passion. Such noble action has its own intrinsic value, irrespective of the outcome. Action is the only thing over which we have control. We have no control over the outcome or the results. The highest level of action is that which is free from attachment to results. We do something because it is worth doing. We act without desire to gain the fruit of our action.

In fact, the action and the fruit of our action are not two separate things: they are part of one single process. Eating food and overcoming hunger are one continuum; drinking water and quenching thirst are two aspects of a single reality. In a similar way, acting to restore ecological balance and finding harmony between Nature and humankind are one and the same. There is no utopia where we can finally achieve perfect peace, total tranquility, everlasting love, or whatever the ideal is. Thus, the change we desire and our action to make that change are integral to each other. Our action is an expression of our love for Nature and for each other. As our love is unconditional and unlimited, so our actions are also unconditional and without an end. What is the fruit of our love? Just love. What is the fruit of our action? More action! Action in the beginning, action in the middle, and action in the end. To live is to act. We need to enjoy our action and find fulfilment in it. No disappointment and no burnout! Activism is not to change the world; activism does change the world.

Mahatma Gandhi said, "Be the change you wish to see in the world." Our actions emerge out of our being. Acting for peace, for sustainability, and for spirituality are a way of being.

The same is true with the practice of the arts. An artist cannot control, nor wish to control, the results. Success or failure are not in the hands of the artist. Practice of art is like prayer or meditation. True prayer doesn't ask for anything. It is simply an offering. Art and activism are the same in this regard. We are in service of the Earth and humanity. We serve until our last breath. Our activism or art is inspired by deep love for humanity and for the Earth. In this view, and from this perspective, art, activism, and love become a permanent way of life. We act out of love not out of desire to succeed. Success is a gift from the universe. If it comes, we are delighted, but if it doesn't come, we don't crave for it, we don't seek it. We are grateful to the universe for choosing us to be the channels of service and activism. With that humility and total inner freedom we act. If we are slaves of our desire for success then we are not free. Our complete and undivided focus should be on our action. Only then can we remain undistracted by our desire for results.

Activism is a journey and not a destination. Through our noble actions, we, the activists, are transformed. Whether anyone else changes or not, we are changed. That in itself is of great value. So let us move from despondency to delight!

Even Jesus Christ and the Buddha could not establish a kingdom of love and compassion on Earth. Would you consider that a failure? No! Their lives and their teachings have enduring value. Their actions stand out as beacons of hope and inspiration to millions of people around the world. Let us be like little Buddhas and act selflessly, with love and compassion.

With all my love,

Satish

PART THREE

Radical Love for Ourselves and Others

*One word frees us of all the weight
and pain of life. That word is love.*

—SOPHOCLES

21

A Love Manifesto

My bounty is as boundless as the sea,
My love is as deep. The more I give thee
The more I have, for both are infinite.

—WILLIAM SHAKESPEARE

Ours is a Love Revolution. Love is logical and magical, simultaneously. The Earth is an embodiment of love. The Earth is our teacher and we learn the art of love from her. The Earth loves us perfectly and, in return, we must learn to love the Earth better.

We say *no* to the policies and practices that harm the Earth and cause global warming, the melting of the arctic ice, and the rise of sea levels. We boycott the businesses and products that harm the planet. We go to prison for the sake of the Earth and we will do so peacefully and happily. We have no fear whatsoever.

We say *yes* to living simply and sustainably. We say yes to planting trillions of trees, and yes to regenerative agriculture. We eat healthy, local, organic, and nutritious foods. We support small farmers and growers around the globe. We live as artisans and artists. We support craftspeople of the world. We resist evil to help dissolve it, and we assist good so that it may flourish.

We never allow despair to diminish our optimism. Activists must be optimists. Pessimism can lead to journalism, but never to activism. With enduring hope and a lifelong commitment, we undertake the journey of transformation. Yes, activism is a journey and not a destination; it is a long-term process and not a short-term product. We urge each other: "Commit yourself to the Earth and live as an artist and an activist." We are all in it together. We have no enemies. The economy of waste and pollution, extraction and exploitation, greed and ego have to be brought to an end through universal participation. Politicians and poets, industrialists and artists, creators and consumers, all of us must join hands and stand together to overcome the perils of pollution and avert the crisis of climate catastrophe.

As we act to bring about outer transformation, we also act for inner transformation. If our minds are polluted by greed, fear, and craving, then we give birth to discontentment, consumerism, and materialism that result in the pollution of the Earth and ourselves. The outer landscape and the inner landscape are two aspects of one reality. Nature out there is not separate from our inner nature.

The old story of division and separation must give way to the new story of unity and connectivity, between the inner and the outer, and between Nature and humans. Meditation and action, intuition and reason, mind and matter, silence and speech, inner and outer, left and right complement each other. Cultivating compassion within and conservation without is the way to embrace the new holistic paradigm.

We heal the wounds caused by the old story of separation and dualism, the prejudice of us and them, the divisions of class, caste, race, religion, identity, and nationality. We apply the balm of unconditional and unlimited love to heal the conflicts among people and between people and the planet.

We transcend divisions and celebrate diversity while embracing the unity of life. We remember that unity is not uniformity. Unity manifests in biodiversity, cultural diversity, truth diversity, diversity of thought and opinion. Evolution favors diversity. From the time of the Big Bang, evolution has worked ceaselessly over billions of years to create diversity in every way. We cherish the diversity of languages, religions, and identities, while remaining united in a total commitment to do no harm to our precious planet; we do no harm to its people, its animals, its forests, and its waters.

We uphold human rights and equally we uphold the rights of Nature; the rights of all living beings. The Earth is not a dead rock, she is Gaia, a living organism. As William Blake said, "Nature is imagination itself." And in the words of Shakespeare, there are "tongues in trees"—yes, trees speak, and we listen. Shakespeare went on to note "books in running brooks … sermons in stones"—yes, we learn to read the books of rivers and of stones. We need not go to temples or churches if we do not wish to; we can hear the teachings of peace, patience, and resilience from the natural world if only we listen.

We do not measure the value of Nature in terms of her usefulness to humans, rather we recognize the intrinsic value of Nature and of the entire Earth. Nature is not simply a resource for the economy, Nature is the source of life itself. We live in harmony with Nature, with the Earth, and with all living beings; with the human and with the other-than-human world. Even when we do not achieve absolute harmony, we maintain that it is an ideal worth striving toward.

We may be called "idealists," but what have the realists achieved in the world? The climate crisis is not the work of idealists. It is the activities of the realists that are causing climate change, the demise of biodiversity, and the pollution of air, water, and soil. Under the watch of the so-called realists' constant hunger for more, wars and other human tragedies have grown exponentially on a global scale. Realists have ruled the world for far too long, and they have made a mess of it. It is high time to give idealists a chance. We are the gentle heroes of our time. Our actions on behalf of the planet and her people are acts of love.

22

Four Obstacles to Love

Love is a deeper season than reason.

—E. E. CUMMINGS

Love is the suspension of doubt. To love, I need to believe in myself and believe wholeheartedly in the people I love. As Tolstoy said, "when you love someone, you love the person as they are, and not as you would like them to be." Four obstacles to love arise because we want people to think, speak, and act in a way that meets our expectations. When they don't, we fall into habits of Criticizing, Complaining, Controlling, and Comparing.

These four C's are destructive obstacles to love.

Criticizing

When we criticize others, we are sitting in judgment. We are effectively saying: I am right and you are wrong. We are saying that there is only one right way and that is my way: I want you to do things my way. This is arrogance. Love and arrogance are like chalk and cheese; they don't go together. Love is the fruit of humility.

Love is not bondage. Love is bonding and belonging. Love is not a merger of two souls. The mathematics of love states that one plus one equals eleven, not two! In the arduous, unpredictable, and marvelous journey of life, love is a promise of companionship. Criticism is a consequence of doubt, doubt in the ability of the other to do the right thing. Allow the light of love to enter our souls and dispel the darkness of doubt. The god of love resides in the temple of trust.

We have been educated to cultivate a critical mind in all circumstances. We have been conditioned to think that doubt is always a good thing. The methodology of Cartesian doubt has been put on a high pedestal and used as the basis of most educational systems.

Critical thinking and the methodology of doubt is useful in the field of philosophy and other intellectual pursuits. But when it comes to love, friendship, and relationships, then criticism needs to be replaced with appreciation. Trust needs to be enshrined in our hearts in place of doubt. Relationships and love grow in the ground of the heart, and the heart is nourished by the nectar of trust.

Doubt deprives us of deep and lasting relationships. Doubt holds us back from making long-term commitments. It is not just in loving relationships that we need to let go of doubt. Even in our working lives, we have to make a commitment to something we love, and pursue our paths in spite of ups and downs, difficulties and obstacles, risks and uncertainties. We must not criticize our own hopes and dreams.

Whether we love gardening or cooking, dancing or singing, farming or manufacturing, we have to ignore the fear of failure and the prospects of success. We must simply trust ourselves and follow our hearts. That is the way of love.

Complaining

When we complain, we are also sitting in judgment. We are saying to others: You have acted carelessly; there is a particular standard of behavior and your actions fall below that standard. We deem their conduct to be irresponsible or objectionable. Complaining is aggressive, and being aggressive is like being a pair of scissors, ready to cut the heart into so many pieces.

Love is not about expectations. Love is about unconditional acceptance of the other as the other is. We are all different and unique. That is so beautiful. The sun of love rises in the dawn of diversity and makes the thousand flowers bloom. Love proclaims: *Vive la différence!*

Complaining stems from an absence of acceptance and a lack of trust. Thus complaining and doubting are bedfellows.

There is room for complaining against social injustice, environmental degradation, racial discrimination, the arms race, and other similar systems of waste, pollution, and violence. In these situations, we are entitled to complain, oppose, and protest, but without hatred and without abusing the upholders of the unjust order. We can and we must stand up for truth, integrity, and beauty. But we must do so with love and compassion in our hearts for those who, in their ignorance, are perpetuating unjust social systems.

Mahatma Gandhi stood up against colonialism and imperialism, but he did so with a great deal of love for the people who were responsible for colonization. Similarly, Martin Luther King Add Jr. was an embodiment of love for those who inflicted the wounds of racism on Black Americans. He used the power of love to campaign vigorously against racism and white supremacy in the United States. Complaining with kindness can be a tall order, and yet it is perfectly possible to do so.

What is appropriate in a social and political context, however, may not be suitable in personal and intimate relationships. In our interactions with friends and family, with colleagues and companions, we need to walk along the path of caring rather than the path of complaining. We all make different kinds of mistakes. Making mistakes is completely normal and natural. The only way to grow is to learn from our mistakes. Learning never stops.

Under the light of love, we swiftly shift from complaining to compassion.

Controlling

The wish to control others is contrary to love. By wishing to control others I am putting myself in a superior position, in a position of ego. Ego is an enemy of love. To be in love, we have to move from ego to eco. As we have seen, *eco* comes from the Greek, which means the house and its family members. When I am truly in love, I am relaxed and at ease. I am unself-conscious. I am home.

In a loving home, there is true mutuality and reciprocity. No one is either inferior or superior. Everyone takes care of each other. In a home, we experience motherly love, fatherly love, brotherly love, sisterly love, romantic love, erotic love, culinary love; there is love of caring and sharing. The ideal home is a control-free zone!

Love is not possessive. Love is liberating. When in love, we participate in the process of living, rather than wishing to be in charge of other people's lives.

Desire to control others is to distrust their ability to self-manage and self-organize. The urge to control others is to deny the truth that everyone is gifted with their own integrity and imagination.

The only constructive and true use of control is control of the self. We can control our anger, our greed, and our ego. Such self-control can free us from conflicts, confrontations, and wars. If we make a shift from control to conciliation, then we can live among others with a sense of community. We can grow in the garden of generosity. We can experience a profound sense of gratitude and grace. We can swim in the sea of love.

Comparing

When we compare one person with another person, we are in the den of dualism. We are caught in the concept of good and bad, right and wrong. As the Sufi poet Rumi urges, "There is a field beyond right and wrong. Let us meet there." That is the field of friendship and unconditional love, where we transcend the tyranny of comparison and fly on the wings of wisdom. Everything has a place, and everything is good in its place.

A tree does not discriminate between a saint and a sinner. It offers its cool shade and fragrant fruit to all and everyone, whoever they are—poor or rich, wise or fool, human or animal, bird or wasp. A tree loves all and compares none. Let us learn how to love from a tree.

Each and every person is unique, a special gift from the universe. When we are in love, we value and celebrate the intrinsic dignity of our beloved ones without comparing them to anyone else. Each and every living being deserves to be appreciated and cherished on their own terms.

We must distinguish in our minds between *having* a lover and *being* a lover. When we wish to have a lover, we are likely to compare one person with another. But when we wish to be a lover, we are more likely to rise above comparisons. Pragmatists compare and contrast. Lovers accept and rejoice. Every kiss is uniquely ecstatic in itself. No two kisses can be compared!

Meditation on the Four Obstacles to Love

May I avoid criticizing, complaining, controlling, and comparing.

Instead, may I practice compassion, consolation, conciliation, and communication.

Furthermore, may I cultivate courtesy and caring.

May I learn to appreciate and to praise others and give thanks for all the gifts of life I receive every day!

23

Walking

Walk as if you are kissing the earth with your feet.

—THICH NHAT HANH

Walking is a metaphor as well as an act. When we "walk the walk," we integrate the ideal with the reality; we bring principles into practice.

There is an implicit connection between such thought and the school of peripatetic philosophers. It was Nietzsche who said, "Don't trust a philosophy which has not been tested by walking." Theologians have their cloisters around a monastic courtyard, and churches and cathedrals have sacred spaces around them for walking while meditating on the mysteries of faith and the metaphysics of existence. Pilgrims go by foot on sacred journeys to reach divine destinations. They walk around the holy peaks of the Himalayas, or to the confluence of sacred rivers, or to the places associated with prophets, poets, and mystics. The act of walking itself is as meaningful for pilgrims as the fact of arrival. Walking is a spiritual action for self-purification, self-transformation, and self-realization.

Environmental, social, and political activists walk in protest against the pollution, exploitation, and injustice perpetuated by those holding the reins of power. Mahatma Gandhi's Salt March to the sea and Martin Luther King's March on Washington were acts of political defiance as well as spiritual awakening. Millions of humans have walked to bring an end to colonialism, racism, sexism, and militarism. To show solidarity with the poor and the oppressed, cultural creatives of all ages, nationalities, and political persuasions have walked to proclaim their support for sustainability, spirituality, justice, peace, freedom, human rights, and the rights of the planet.

My teacher and mentor Vinoba Bhave walked a hundred thousand miles across the length and breadth of India over fifteen years, persuading wealthy landowners to share their property with the landless laborers in the name of love and justice. It was a miracle that he was able to open the hearts of these landowners and collect four million acres of land in gifts, which he then distributed among the dispossessed and deprived. It was his walk that inspired and impressed the wealthy to part with their land. He claimed he walked because he was "moved by love."

My own mother was a great walker as well. She had a smallholding, a small farm about an hour's walk from our house in Rajasthan. Our family was blessed with a horse and a camel, but Mother never rode on animals. She would always go on foot to reach the farm. Our religious tradition, Jainism, required us to respect animals and not inflict any undue suffering or hardship upon them. If someone suggested that my mother ride on a horse she would smile and simply reply, "How would you like it if the horse wanted to ride you?"

I would often walk with my mother to the farm or on errands. As we walked, she told stories and sang songs. She pointed out the miracles of Nature that most people took for granted. Walking, for my mother, was a source of joy and an act of love.

And so it is for me. In my early childhood I became a Jain monk. I walked barefoot for nine years, never traveling by car, train, plane, or boat. I did not even use a bicycle. My feet became wide and firm. I walked on sand and pebbles, in heat and in cold, without socks, sandals, or shoes. And yet in my mind I felt that I was walking on rose petals. My guru said to me, "Practice gratitude toward the Earth who holds you on her back and enables you to walk." This was his way of teaching me a lesson in Earth spirituality. "People plough the Earth, they tread upon her, dig holes in her body, and yet the Earth forgives. She is so generous that if you plant one seed, she returns a thousand fruits. So, meditate on the unconditional love of the Earth and practice the same kind of compassion, generosity, and forgiveness in your own life."

I eventually left the Jain monastic order, but not my love of walking. In 1962, along with my friend E. P. Menon, I embarked upon a Pilgrimage for Peace, walking from New Delhi to Moscow, to Paris, to London, and to Washington, DC. We walked eight thousand miles without a penny in our pockets. Whether we were able to bring more peace to the world or not, I certainly found peace within myself through walking. I learned to trust myself, to trust strangers, and to trust the world. I gained confidence and resilience. I was able to let go of my fears of the unknown, unplanned, and uncertain. I grew to love mountains, forests, and deserts equally. I appreciated wind and rain, snow and sunshine with equanimity. I faced hostility and hospitality both with humor and acceptance. I learned to expect nothing and accept everything as it comes. When there is no expectation, there is no disappointment. Walking, for me, became a source of self-realization. Now, walking is more than a way to move from one place to another: it is a way of life, and a way to health, harmony, and happiness.

When I was fifty, I went on a second pilgrimage around the British Isles. From Devon to Somerset then Dorset and on along the Pilgrims' Way to Canterbury. I walked from village to village and from town to town, immersing myself in the beauty of the British landscape. Then along the east coast I arrived at the holy isle of Lindisfarne, where the Celtic saints of ancient times meditated on Nature while wading in the sea.

I walked across Scotland and reached Iona, one of the most peaceful places I have ever been, then along the west coast, down to Wales and back through the West Country and over Exmoor, and finally home to Hartland. It was a sacred journey over four months and two thousand miles, in which I enjoyed incredible hospitality from people of all backgrounds. Once again, I walked without any money in my pocket and encountered many miracles emerging out of the sheer generosity and goodness of ordinary men and women, whom I would meet for the first and only time during my journey.

I am now in my eighties, and it is thanks to walking that I do not lack energy, enthusiasm, or passion. My immune system is robust. I have never taken any form of antibiotics, and have only ever been hospitalized due to a single broken bone.

People ask me the secret of my good health. My answer is plain and simple: I love walking. It is good for my body, good for my mind, and good for my spirit. I walk for an hour or so every day and, failing that, I go for a constitutional stroll after my meal. Walking is digestive, refreshing, and calming. No words are sufficient to contain my praise for walking. I choose to move and flow rather than to remain fixed and static.

I often call to mind the words of John Muir: "In every walk with Nature one receives far more than one seeks." When we walk, we cultivate a deep understanding of the natural world. We fall in love with Nature, which enables us to experience her deeply, and this, in turn, prompts us to make a deep commitment to her care. We celebrate her, and act to protect her. This is the process of learning a Deep Ecology. I walk on Earth, and I walk for Earth.

Walking meditation is a magnificent spiritual practice. And for those of us who wish to put a lighter footprint on the planet, walking is the simplest and easiest way to reduce our carbon contribution to the atmosphere. So let us walk to our offices, walk to shops, walk to schools, walk to churches. If anyone claims that they don't have time to walk, I would like to remind them that there is no shortage of time. The time we measure in hours, days, weeks, and months is only for the sake of convenience. In reality, time is infinite.

24

Food and Garden

Life begins the day you start a garden.

—A CHINESE PROVERB

My mother had a five-acre field, which she called her "garden of love." She grew melons, millet, mung dhal, and sesame, in addition to various vegetables. As I mentioned, she would take me walking with her to the field, where I would help her sow the seeds, water the plants, and harvest the crops.

She was also a very good cook. "Food is medicine as well as a source of nutrition," my mother would say. She encouraged me to work with her, as she made chapatis, an unleavened flat bread, or dhal and vegetables with ginger, turmeric, coriander, cumin, and cardamom. Ever since, I have enjoyed gardening and cooking. When I was living in a Gandhian ashram in Bodh Gaya, in North India, our motto was "Those who eat must participate in growing food, and those who grow food must have enough to eat." The Gandhian principle of food is that there should be as short a distance as possible between the soil where it is grown and the mouths that it feeds. If the food is coming from your own garden, or a local farmers market, then the food is fresh. If food is transported long distances and packaged in plastic, it cannot be as fresh as it should be. In short, we must think globally but eat locally.

In 1982, I established the Small School in Hartland, England. The very first day when children, parents, and teachers gathered I asked how our school would be different from other schools. The answer was that every day at our school, the children and teachers would prepare their lunches, say grace, and eat good food together. The rationale for this is simple: you cannot provide a good education on a bad diet. It is no good learning about Darwin and Shakespeare, science and history if we don't even know how to feed ourselves. So learning to grow, learning to cook, and learning to eat together are as important in education as learning to read and write.

Many schools have food brought to them by mass suppliers over long distances. The food is often tasteless. A significant amount is wasted, as children do not enjoy it, and then they go out and buy junk food full of sugar and salt. While perhaps tastier, it is not nutritious in the least. On the contrary, it is quite harmful to our children, leading to obesity, learning and memory problems, and even depression. Young people leave universities with BA, MA, or PhD degrees, but many of them don't know how to prepare a proper meal. Schools have swimming pools, sports halls, and science labs, but very few have gardens and kitchens where teachers and students can grow and cook their own food together. In my view, all schools should have gardens and kitchens. Why do we give so little attention to food when it is a fundamental need for a good life?

In 1991, I established Schumacher College for adult education, and there too I applied the same principles. All students and participants are invited and encouraged to work in the garden and kitchen. When students choose to do so, they are not missing lessons because gardening and cooking are the lesson.

The garden at Schumacher College is truly a Garden of Love, something celebrated by one course in particular that I find most inspiring. The Growers Program, which provides students with six months of intensive gardening, was designed to train young people in the art of regenerative agriculture and gardening, and to show that there are many perfectly viable and productive options to grow food sustainably, with meaning and love. While doing so, they also produce wholesome food for the college. It was calculated that the college kitchen saved twenty thousand pounds in one year alone on produce from the efforts of our fifteen Growers, who cultivated seven acres of land with exemplary love, passion, and pleasure.

Industrial farming, factory farming, meat production, and agribusiness presently contribute 25 to 30 percent of the greenhouse gases that cause global warming. The amount of water and electricity used to grow the world's food supply through modern methods of farming is colossal. The ways such farming depletes and erodes precious soil are beyond measure. The consequences of such farming on the natural environment are disastrous, while the quality of food produced through such systems is substandard at best. The effects of producing and consuming such food on human health are a matter of grave concern, yet we continue to perpetuate factory farming as if there is no alternative.

Agroecology is gathering strength and attracting the attention of those who wish to grow good food sustainably by following the way of regenerative agriculture. The best way to do this is to move away from the monoculture of crops or meat production on an industrial scale and to incorporate the principle of biodiversity into agriculture. Growing trees, grains, flowers, fruits, and vegetables side by side is the essential principle of agroecology. Diversity maintains the fertility of the soil and builds resilience in crops.

Due to the industrialized and mechanized nature of farming, we have become disconnected from the soil. Through agroecology, we reconnect with the soil and with our roots. Still, people doubt if such sustainable methods of agriculture could produce enough food to feed the growing population of the world. This is a result of a mistaken belief that food can be grown without people being involved in the process of producing food. We all need to eat, but we don't seem to want to involve ourselves in growing food. We want machines, computers, and even robots to cheaply produce our food and distribute it globally. This has been and will remain the way of increasing the carbon emissions causing our present climate catastrophe. If we wish to feed people properly without adding to the climate crisis, then more of us need to be involved in the production of food. And why not? After all, food is life. Food is sacred.

To respond to the crisis of climate chaos and embrace regenerative and sustainable systems of food production, we need to restore the dignity of working on the land. Cultivating the soil and producing food is a noble vocation and a respected profession. Food is not merely a commercial commodity, food is a source of life, and a sacred gift of the Earth. Working on the land as a gardener or a farmer is good for our physical as well as our spiritual well-being.

The diet is vegetarian at Schumacher College. We believe that compassion for animals is the foundation to developing compassion in our hearts for humans and for all living beings. Moreover, feeding a person a plant-based diet requires just one acre of land, whereas feeding a person a meat-based diet requires five acres. Animals are increasingly kept in factory farms and slaughterhouses where water consumption is immense, and where many animals never see daylight their entire lives. These unhappy animals are consumed by humans. How can people be happy eating the meat of unhappy animals? My advice to people who eat meat is to eat less and only if it comes from free-range animals, who have lived good and happy lives. And for any willing to become vegetarians, so much the better. If food is well prepared, if it is fresh and delicious, we will not miss the meat.

Once I was invited to a primary school to speak about the environment. After my talk, I had a conversation with a curious pupil, who began by asking my favorite animal. "The elephant," I replied. The pupil asked me why, and I explained that the elephant is so big and strong, and yet it is a vegetarian animal, which shows that to be big and strong we don't have to eat meat. Intrigued, the pupil asked which was my second favorite animal, to which I replied, "the horse." Again, the pupil wanted to know why and I obliged, reminding that horses are so powerful that we measure the power of an engine in "horsepower," yet horses are also vegetarians. "From now on I will be a vegetarian," the pupil responded, already feeling a little bigger and stronger.

It is a complete myth that we will not have enough strength if we don't consume meat. My family are followers of the Jain religion and the Jains have been strict vegetarians for more than two thousand years. Many of my family members, myself included, have lived a healthy life well into our eighties and nineties.

Vegetarian food should ideally be organic as well. Chemicals are often the product of crude oil that is drilled from thousands of feet underground, and it is this fossil fuel that generates greenhouse gases, which contribute to global warming. If produce and grains are grown with chemical fertilizers using fossil fuels, and then transported long distances again using more fossil fuels, then the damage to the environment diminishes the benefit of vegetarianism. Food being local, vegetarian, and organic is a continuum we must strive to respect.

We must also never entertain the idea of using genetically modified seeds produced by multinational companies such as Monsanto. Seeds have evolved over thousands of years to suit the conditions of the soil, the climate, and the environment.

Genetically engineered and modified seeds are developed quickly in laboratory conditions. These commercial seeds are developed with the desire to make a big profit, with no regard for costs to the environment or human health.

For traditional farmers, the seed is sacred—it is a source of life. Each farmer is self-reliant in saving their seeds, whereas a commercial company like Monsanto views seeds as merely a commodity to buy and sell for profit and to keep farmers dependent on the companies. Thus genetically modified seeds are also undemocratic. They take away the freedom of the farmers to save their own seeds. The illusion is that genetically modified seeds produce larger crops, and while the crop size may increase, the nutritional value actually decreases. It is better for all to eat nutritious food in smaller quantities than modified and unhealthy food in large quantities.

Let us grow our wholesome food lovingly and locally. Let it be largely vegetarian, organic, and free from genetic modification. Let us eat our food lovingly in small quantities, and in the company of our friends and family. Love of food is the celebration of food and not the indulgence in food. I share food with others as an expression of my love for them. A good meal expresses love louder than words.

25

Simplicity

Great acts are made up of small deeds.

—LAO TZU

Love of simplicity is the prerequisite for sustainability, spirituality, social harmony, and peace.

The Jain faith places the principle of *aparigraha* second only to *ahimsa*. It is a very beautiful word, but not easy to translate. It means a freedom from the bondage of material possessions. It is an ecological principle. It is a principle of reduction in consumption, of minimal accumulation of material possessions. If we can manage with three or four shirts, then why have ten or twenty? After all, we can only wear one shirt at a time. Why do we need to accumulate a cupboard full of shoes when a few will do? And so on for every material possession. Jains are required to use material objects to meet their needs and not their greed. In practicing aparigraha, one is freed from the burden, worry, and anxiety of owning too much stuff.

This principle of non-accumulation is just the opposite to our modern idea of the economy, where maximization of production and maximization of consumption is the driving ideal. Even at the time of religious festivals, such as Christmas and Easter, shopping and consumption take priority over any religious rituals. People become so *consumed* with buying and selling that they are left with very little or no time for their spiritual nourishment. No time for themselves, no time for reflection or to practice an art or craft.

Consumerism clutters our homes, our lives, and our workplaces. Our wardrobes are full of these unworn clothes, shoes, jackets, and so on. In our kitchens, things sit in cupboards hardly used, yet we hold on to them thinking that one day they will be useful, even if that day rarely comes. It is the same story on our desks, where papers, files, and books pile up day after day to clutter the space. We have become habituated to accumulate and store. When we look at our attics, at our bedrooms, at our closets, we find clutter everywhere.

The problem is far more serious than mere wasted space. All these material goods have to come from somewhere, from the Earth, and thus from Nature. Mass extraction, mass production, mass distribution, and mass consumption result in waste and pollution on a global scale. If we want to love Nature and be serious about sustainability, then we have to change our habits of accumulating unnecessary possessions in our homes and workplaces, and learn the art of living well with less.

If the many billions of people on this planet were to accumulate, consume, and then waste and pollute as Europeans and Americans do, we would need three planets and perhaps more to accommodate it all. The fact is that we have only one planet, such that simplicity—living simply and making a small footprint on the Earth—is a sustainability imperative.

Many of the goods we accumulate are cheaply made in countries where labor is inexpensive, like China or Bangladesh. We buy them and soon get bored with them, so we throw them away, and the landfills get crammed full. By contrast, simplicity considers elegance and beauty with each acquisition. Whatever we have should be beautiful, useful, and durable at the same time.

As my mother used to say, "Have few things but have beautiful things, so that you can cherish them, use them, and wear them with pleasure." This traditional wisdom was once common sense, but sadly such sense is no longer common.

Love of simplicity is also a prerequisite for spirituality. For our personal well-being, we need to have time for ourselves so that we can meditate, practice yoga or tai chi, read poetry or books of spiritual teaching, and be at ease within ourselves. To acquire gadgets and possessions, we work long and hard to earn money, and then we have to spend our remaining time shopping around and spending that money. In the end, we are lucky if we have time to enjoy the stuff we have accumulated. And yet we complain that we have no time for ourselves, for our spiritual well-being, for imaginative work, for reading or writing poetry, for painting or gardening, for listening to music, or taking a walk.

Cluttered homes create cluttered minds. If we live simply, we need less money. Freed from the need to work more, our time will be liberated from drudgery and boring routine. We can pursue the path of spiritual fulfilment; we can focus on personal well-being and on the development of arts, crafts, and our imaginations. We can dedicate time and space to friendship and to love. It is a beautiful paradox: material minimalism maximizes spiritual and ecological well-being.

Simplicity is also a prerequisite for social justice. If a few of us have too much, others invariably have too little. We need to live simply so that others may simply live. Some want the luxuries of more than one house, more than one car, more than one computer, more of everything. Such inequality represents injustice and creates envy and social discord. I have known people with extraordinary luxuries, and they are no happier than those who live a much simpler life. Happiness lies not in the possession of things. Happiness lies in contentment of the heart. When one knows that enough is enough, one always has enough, and when one doesn't know this, however much one has is never enough.

When I speak of simplicity, I don't mean a life of depravation, hair shirt living, and hardship. I believe in a good life, in beautiful things, in arts and crafts, and in sufficiency. I believe in joy and celebration. In fact, I prioritize elegance before simplicity, which I believe is and should always be elegant by nature. We should all have a comfortable and pleasant life. But currently our complicated lives are no longer comfortable. We sacrifice comfort for the sake of convenience, the pursuit of which has led us astray.

Far too many are denied comfort altogether. If we are blessed with wealth, we can use it for philanthropy, for caring for the Earth and her people. Loving simplicity requires attention, awareness, and mindfulness. "Any fool can make things complicated. It requires a genius to make things simple," said E. F. Schumacher. And we all have that innate genius within us. The only thing we need to do is pay attention and discover our genius to live well by living simply.

The economics of extravagance leads to war. The economics of simplicity leads to peace. When we seek ever higher living standards and ever greater economic growth, we seek to monopolize our natural resources. We go to war for oil, for land, and for other resources.

From Leo Tolstoy to Mahatma Gandhi, all great social reformers and writers have shown the path of peace by living and practicing simplicity. As Tolstoy said in his great book *War and Peace:* "There is no greatness where there is no simplicity, goodness, and truth."

26

Reason and Science

You can't blame gravity for falling in love.

—ALBERT EINSTEIN

Humanity is on a journey, a journey from separation to relationship, from lust to love, and from dualism to unity. One of the dominant dualisms of our time has been the disconnection between science and spirituality, between reason and love. Since the age of pure reason, our educational system has been working hard to establish the conviction that science must be free of spirituality, and that spirituality should have nothing to do with science. In other words, reason must rule while love is relegated to the personal realm.

For the past hundred years, millions of graduates have been leaving universities inducted into the belief that spirituality is a matter of private life, if not something to be dismissed altogether. And yet this tendency has ignored past and present scientists who see no dichotomy between the scientific and the spiritual, between love and reason.

The outstanding German poet and scientist Johann Wolfgang Goethe worked with a profound scientific spirit. In his books *Metamorphosis of Plants* and *Theory of Colors*, he challenged a narrow and linear view of science. With his phenomenological understanding of Nature, he expounded a more interrelated, cyclical, and holistic science. But Goethe's idealistic and spiritual science has been neglected by students of science in most universities. Instead, he has been valued as a great poet and not as a scientist.

The same is true of Leonardo da Vinci, who is remembered as a great artist but rarely as an influential scientist. Because he was concerned with living forms and embraced the science of quality as well as quantity, our contemporary science of complexity and systems thinking finds its roots in da Vinci's work. The moment we think of a science of quality, the spiritual comes into play.

Albert Einstein was also a spiritual scientist. He said, "Everyone who is seriously involved in the pursuit of science becomes convinced that a spirit is manifest in the laws of the universe and in the face of which we, humans, with our modest powers, must feel humble." Einstein respected the religious dimension of human experience, claiming that "science without religion is blind and religion without science is lame." He was not talking about organized religious establishments; he was talking about religious experience, which is beyond measurement and institutional dogmas.

Bringing spirituality and science, love and reason together helps to bring meaning and measurement together. These two should not be fragmented or separated. A sense of unmanifested wonder and curiosity, of intuition and inspiration exists before empirical knowledge from the experimentation, evidence, and proof that lead to scientific hypotheses and theories. Dismissing unmanifest intuition or inspiration, as some materialist scientists do, is a grave folly.

The word *spirit* simply means breath, or wind. We cannot see, touch, or measure the wind, but we can feel it. As a tree's limbs are moved by wind, humans are moved by spirit. Breath, or wind, is the invisible and subtle force that makes life possible. The visible is sustained by the invisible. Outer material reality is held together through the power of inner, spiritual reality. Acknowledging one and denying the other is like wanting a bird to fly with just one wing.

The reality of wholeness is composed of two interrelated aspects. Chinese call it the harmony of yin and yang. Indians call it the balance of Shiva and Shakti. Positive and negative, dark and light, silence and speech, emptiness and fullness, spirit and matter—the unmanifest and the manifest are part of one single whole.

Uniting science and spirituality has a very practical purpose. Science without spirituality can easily lose an ethical perspective. Scientists without the guidance of spirituality have engaged in the invention of nuclear bombs and other weapons of war, genetic engineering, artificial intelligence, factory farming in which animals are reared in cruel conditions, and technologies that create waste, pollution, and destruction of the natural world. Science without the guidance of spiritual values is responsible for many of the problems that the world faces today. Science needs the helping hand of spiritual wisdom in order to maintain its integrity and modify its power. Science by itself is not benign, value-free, or neutral. Without spiritual wisdom, science can be dangerous. It can be subject to manipulation by the wealthy and politically powerful.

As science needs spirituality, spirituality also needs science. Without science, spirituality can easily and quickly turn into blind faith, dogmatism, sectarianism, and fundamentalism. Unscientifically minded people too easily claim: "My god is the only true god and I have the truth. Everybody must be converted to my truth." Such narrow religious exclusivity has also led to wars, conflicts, terrorism, and division. Science helps to keep our minds open so we can seek truth and act for the benefit of the whole of humanity and for the good of all living beings, human and other-than-human.

Do we want to live in a fragmented way, either as materialists discarding the subjective dimension of spiritual wisdom or as spiritual seekers denigrating the objective world of scientific discovery? The choice is ours. I suggest we embrace spirituality with scientific minds. For me, science and spirituality are complementary parts of the whole. Science is built on reason, and spirituality is built on love.

According to the well-known neurologist Iain McGilchrist, our brains have two hemispheres. The left hemisphere is the place of science and the right hemisphere is the place of spirit, intuition, and love. In his book, *The Master and His Emissary*, McGilchrist says that the right hemisphere of the spirit is and should be the dominant force, while the left hemisphere of science and reason is and should be the emissary. Enduring love is achieved through the union of the two hemispheres of the brain.

But influenced by the workings of our social, economic, and political lives, and even supported through modern education, we have come to privilege the left hemisphere and suppress the right. The emissary rules while the master is imprisoned!

Science and reason are about theory and measurement. Spirituality is about implicit and internal reality. Science looks at the world and sees its various parts in fragments. Spirituality looks at the world and sees it whole. Science considers the Earth, Nature, and even the human body in mechanical terms. Spirituality views them all as living organisms.

From a holistic and nondualistic perspective, we need both sides. We need to have the left hemisphere of our brains as active as the right hemisphere. We are born with two incredible gifts. What sense is there to cherish only one or the other?

Let us restore the spiritual qualities of love, compassion, humility, and mutuality to our education system, and to our social, economic, and political worlds. And let us allow science, reason, measurement, and mathematics to inform our religious, spiritual, and emotional worlds.

The question is, where do we start? How do we ensure that there is no fragmentation between love and reason, between science and spirituality? The answer is education. We have to start with our children. At home and at school, in colleges and in universities, we must introduce the big picture, the whole story: inner and outer, spiritual and material, love and reason, heart and head. Let us bring love back into education.

27

Learning

Education is the kindling of a flame,
not the filling of a vessel.

—SOCRATES

Modern education primarily promotes absorption of information, then, to a lesser extent, knowledge; unfortunately, there is little room or opportunity in our schools and universities to include experience and wisdom, spirituality and love.

It is believed that a student is an empty vessel and the responsibility of the teacher is to fill the empty vessel with as much useful information as possible. This is a mistaken interpretation of education. The word education comes from the Latin *educo*, which means to "lead forth" or to "take out," and the implication is that one who educates takes out what is already there, one leads forth what is dormant. To educate is to make explicit what is already implicit.

We might compare a student with a seed. A tree is already in the seed. A gardener or an orchard keeper or a forester does not teach the seed how to become a tree. The work of a gardener is to provide the right soil and conditions, so that the seed is able to self-realize and become the tree. Students have the same innate potential to become who they are as they mature. The work of an educator and thus our educational institutions is to provide students with encouragement, as well as environments and conditions conducive to self-discovery and self-realization.

Education should not be for self-promotion or self-interest; education is not about getting a good job so that we can buy a big house, a nice car, and other material possessions for our comfort. Education is not for enhancing the ego or fueling the desire for name, fame, status, recognition, power, and position for ourselves. Education is a journey of self-discovery and self-realization in the service of the human community and the Earth. Every member of the human community benefits from reciprocity and mutuality because we are all related, we are all connected.

Modern education creates adults who lack the skills and confidence to be resilient and self-reliant, and to serve selflessly. Modern education creates job seekers and employees. The jobs they do are mostly minding machines or shifting papers. Even farmers no longer have to touch the soil and seeds, or harvest the crops and milk the cows with their own hands.

Most of manufacturing has gone the same way. Machines have replaced human hands, and in this robotic age we are facing the prospect of robots increasingly replacing humans. Modern education is not only responsible for deskilling but also for dehumanizing.

In order to evolve from information to knowledge and from experience to wisdom, which is the purpose of true education, we need to introduce the idea of learning by doing. We need to use our heads, hearts, and hands to gain knowledge and undergo life-changing experiences. Wisdom arises where knowledge and experience meet. The task of education is not to produce ever-increasing numbers of consumers, but to help humans to become makers and creators, poets and artists by developing skills and techniques and by encouraging the use of their intuitions and imaginations. As the American journalist Sydney Harris once said, "the purpose of education is to turn mirrors into windows."

Therefore, let there be a garden in every school and every college, so that young people may learn how to grow food. Students and teachers should be offered facilities and possibilities to prepare their own lunches with wholesome and fresh ingredients, so that school meals become occasions for building community and developing a sense of belonging. We must offer all young people opportunities to learn crafts, such as pottery, woodwork, weaving, mending, and repairing. The status of making and crafting should be equal to the status of science, math, and literature. That is the way of learning by doing. As it has been said, "tell me and I forget, teach me and I may remember, involve me and I will learn."

It is time to wake up and rediscover the meaning of education again, to transform it into a pilgrimage of self-discovery.

This can happen only when we are prepared to embrace uncertainties, ambiguities, difficulties, and hardships. Only when we have problems can we use our imaginations to solve them, rather than running away from them. In the comfort of the classroom we can obtain information, in the luxury of libraries we can gain knowledge, but experience can be gained only when we are out in the storm of life and in the unpredictable terrain of Nature.

Technology is seductive and a double-edged sword. It can be a useful tool to connect, or it can be a brutal weapon to control. If technology is the servant and if it is used with wisdom to enhance human relationships, without polluting the environment or wasting natural resources, then it can be good. But if technology becomes the master, and human creativity and ecological integrity are sacrificed at its altar, then technology becomes a curse of our own making.

Some of the champions of digital technology have been promoting the idea of transforming face-to-face learning to a system of education rooted in internet technology, and operated by remote control, thereby integrating digital technology, fully and permanently, into the educational process. In doing so, the opportunity for personal relationships and intimate interactions between students and teachers is removed.

Every human being comes into this world with their own unique potential. No two seeds grow into the same tree. The work of a true teacher is to observe and spot that special spiritual quality in a child and help to nurture it and enhance it with care, attention, and empathy. Thus, the beautiful idea of education is to maintain human diversity, cultural diversity, and diversity of talents through decentralized, democratic, human-scale, spiritualized, and personalized systems of schooling. How can we trust a computer to "bring forth" what is innate and unique to any particular human child?

A good school is a community of learners in which education is not predetermined by remote authorities; rather, it is a journey of exploration where students, teachers, and parents work together to discover right ways to relate to the world and find meaningful ways of moving through it together. Thus, education is an improvised emergent act.

The idea of digital learning through remote control and predetermined curriculums moves away from the rich and holistic ideal of education entirely. Digital teaching looks at children as if they were identical empty vessels in need of being filled with external information. The quality of information or knowledge given to the child remotely and digitally is determined centrally by people who have a vested interest in a particular outcome. And that outcome is largely to turn humans into instruments to run the money machine, and to increase the profitability of big corporations.

Such centralized and depersonalized systems of digital education destroy diversity and impose uniformity; they destroy community culture and impose corporate culture; they destroy cultural diversity and impose a monoculture.

A computer cannot teach kindness. Only in a real learning community can children ascertain how to be loving, how to be kind, how to be compassionate, and how to be respectful. In a school community, children learn together, play together, eat together, and laugh together. If they are fortunate, they produce plays and perform concerts together. They go on field trips together. It is through these shared human activities that children gain a deep appreciation of life. Education is more than the acquisition of information and facts; education is a living experience. Sitting in front of a computer for hours is no way to learn social skills, an ecological worldview, or spiritual values.

Placing the future of our children in the hands of a few digital giants like Google, Microsoft, and Amazon and placing such companies in charge of educational systems is a recipe for a digital dictatorship that opens the doors to disaster. If democratic societies are opposed to military dictatorship, then why should they embrace corporate dictatorship, let alone supply their own children? Through smart technologies, these giant corporations are able to trace and exploit every activity of our children, and later, when they are adults, through algorithms and data manipulation, they can be controlled. We have already experienced the way algorithms, artificial intelligence, biotechnology, nanotechnology, and other forms of so-called smart technologies have been used to control, manipulate, and undermine democratic values. The techno giants who consider humans as "biohazards" cannot be trusted with the future of our children. How could we permit such a dystopian reality to emerge?

Rather than investing in virtual technology, our societies should invest in people. We should be investing in more teachers, in smaller schools. We should aim for smaller class sizes and bottom-up, imaginative, benign, and appropriate technology. Our children need to learn not only about

Nature but from Nature. They need to learn from forests and farming, from permaculture and agriculture, from agroecology and organic gardening, from marine life and wildlife. Such knowledge and skills cannot be learned by staring at a computer screen. Technology and science have a role in education, but let us keep them in their place and not allow them to dominate our lives and the lives of our children.

We are moving into a new age: the Age of Ecology. Therefore, we need to rebalance the education system accordingly. By focusing on a holistic educational paradigm, we will be able to serve ecology and economy together, love and reason together, science and spirituality together. Thus, we make education fit for generations to come.

28

Generosity

You often say, "I would give, but only to the deserving."
The trees in your orchard say not so, nor the flocks in your pasture.
They give that they may live, for to withhold is to perish.

—KHALIL GIBRAN

Generosity is abandonment of fear; fear on the part of the giver and on the part of the receiver as well. My most direct experiences of generosity occurred across cultures and continents during my eight-thousand-mile walk for peace, which began at the grave of Mahatma Gandhi in New Delhi and ended at the grave of John F. Kennedy in Washington, DC. Traveling on foot and without money, I had no choice but to let go of my fears and trust in my heart that people who didn't know me would give me food and shelter, love and blessings day after day for more than two years.

At the border of India and Pakistan, one of my dearest friends, Kranti, came to me, and she offered me some packets of food.

"At least you should take this with you," she said. "You are entering Pakistan. We are still in a state of war. In the minds of many people there, India is an enemy country. Please take some food, take some money, in case you need it."

"My dear friend," I said, "one of the purposes of our pilgrimage is to make peace among enemies and experience the generosity of ordinary people. If I carry food to Pakistan then effectively I am carrying fear in my heart. Fear leads to wars. To make peace, I must trust. The packets of food you are giving me are not just packets of food, they are packets of fear and mistrust."

"You are going through Muslim countries," she said, sobbing. "Christian countries, communist countries, capitalist countries, unknown places, unknown languages, high mountains, vast deserts, fierce forests, and freezing snow! How are you going to survive without money and without food? I don't know if I will ever see you again!"

"People are people everywhere," I said, trying to reassure my friend. "And people are generous. But if occasionally I don't get food, then I will treat that day as an opportunity to fast. I will enjoy hunger! If sometimes I don't get shelter for the night, I will sleep under the million-star hotel; surely this would be better than a five-star hotel! Most of all, I have faith in people. I will be fine. Give me your blessings. Give me a hug."

As soon as we came out of border control in Pakistan, to our utter surprise, we were stopped by a young man who introduced himself as Gulam Yasin. He asked if we were the two Indians who were walking for peace through Pakistan on a mission of goodwill.

"Yes, we are," I replied, "but how did you come to know about us and our walk for peace? We don't know anyone in Pakistan, and we have written to no one. And yet here you are."

"Your story has traveled ahead of you. When I heard about you, I thought, well, I am for peace too, and I want to offer them my hospitality. I have come to greet you and receive you. Welcome to Pakistan."

We had only just stepped foot in Pakistan and already we experienced a genuine gesture of generosity. We were being welcomed by a complete stranger. Gulam Yasin told us that he lived sixteen miles away in Lahore, and offered to drive us to his home where we would be his guests for as long as we liked. We thanked him but insisted on walking and meeting him there despite the scorching heat. He tried to change our minds, but we explained that we were walking the entire journey as a personal commitment to ourselves. We assured him we would see him at the designated meeting spot that evening, and at last he relented.

As we headed toward Lahore I said to Menon, "If we come here as Indians, we meet Pakistanis; if we come here as Hindus, we meet Muslims, but if we come as human beings, we meet human beings everywhere we go. During this pilgrimage, the cosmos is our country, the Earth is our home, and humanity is our religion."

As promised, Gulam Yasin met us at the gate of the beautiful Shalimar Gardens. The evening sun was a ball of fire setting behind the majestic Friday Mosque. The air was filled with the fragrance of jasmine flowers. The generosity of Nature was met only by the generous heart of our new friend.

While we were walking into town, Gulam Yasin had been busy inviting his friends, apparently telling them all about the arrival of two idealistic Indians, who had set off to walk around the world for peace. A number of his friends and family members gathered at his home for a wonderful feast of vegetarian food, even though the Yasin family was not vegetarian. Saffron rice with sultanas, almonds, and cardamom, naan freshly baked in a tandoor oven, peas and potatoes cooked in onion, garlic, and tomato sauce, and other delicious dishes were served. I surveyed the table and smiling faces around me that evening, noting the superbly generous hospitality we were receiving on our very first day out of India in a so-called enemy land.

And in the twenty-eight months that followed, while we were on the road, we were looked after with the utmost kindness by strangers in their yurts at 11,000 feet in the Hindu Kush mountains of Afghanistan, in the mud huts of small villages set around the oases in the deserts of Iran, in the snow-covered country cottages of Armenia and Georgia, in the warm farmhouses of Russia, in the high-rise apartments of Moscow, and on to the bustling cities and suburbs of Europe. Whether we were in Berlin or Bonn, in Paris or London, in New York or DC, it was the innate generosity of the human heart that sustained us in all these places, despite the fact that we were walking during the height of the Cold War. We were hosted in private homes, in youth hostels, in hospitals, in police stations, in churches, and in student dormitories. Everywhere we went, we were met with generous hospitality by people whom we would never see again and who expected nothing in return. This selfless giving was not the exception on our journey, but the rule. Trust begets trust. Love begets love.

When we are born, we are naked and utterly vulnerable. And yet the benevolent universe, in its generosity, placed milk in the breast of our mothers, along with the will to protect and nurture their babies. Our mothers carry us in their wombs for nine months. They suffer great labor pains to bring us into this world. They breastfeed us the early years of our lives. What better example of generosity of spirit can we call upon? All because of love. Every mother is a hero. For me, motherhood is synonymous with generosity; it is our living example of selfless generosity, and mothers are the embodiment of unconditional love. We need to express our gratitude to our mothers and pay homage to them by acknowledging their generosity of spirit.

Generosity is not only a human quality. Every day I am amazed to witness the generosity of Nature. I planted an apple seedling thirty years ago. That tiny plant has become a beautiful tree and has been giving me hundreds of apples, year after year, for the past twenty-five years. The tree never asks me for anything in return. I learn lessons of unconditional love and generosity from trees.

Fruit, flowers, grains, herbs, and vegetables of thousands of varieties, colors, aromas, and shapes feed us and nourish us day after day. They grow out of the generosity of the humble soil. And yet far too many humans, either in our ignorance or in our arrogance, take Nature for granted. Let us realize the truth of Nature's generosity and express our gratitude. Thank you trees, thank you soil, thank you rain, thank you sunshine, thank you Mother Nature, thank you goddess Gaia.

Mutuality and reciprocity are the foundation stones of the house of generosity. As I have received so much from strangers, from my ancestors, and from Nature, I wish to be generous to any strangers who come my way. I wish to be generous to coming generations and leave good things for them. And I wish to return something to Nature by way of planting trees, building soil in my garden, and practicing regenerative forms of food production such as permaculture and agroecology.

May all living beings upon this Earth, humans and other-than-humans, live well, live peacefully, find fulfilment, and be self-realized. May we cultivate such generosity of spirit in our hearts for the whole of humanity and for the entire planet.

As Pablo Picasso said, "The purpose of life is to give it away."

29

Ten Ways to Love

Listen without interrupting
Share without pretending
Speak without accusing
Enjoy without complaining
Give without sparing
Trust without wavering
Pray without ceasing
Forgive without punishing
Answer without arguing
Promise without forgetting

—ANONYMOUS

ACKNOWLEDGMENTS

First of all, my deepest gratitude goes to June Mitchell, my beloved wife and life companion for more than fifty years, who has helped me tremendously in writing *Radical Love*. I wish to express my profound appreciation to Claire and Roger Ash-Wheeler who offered me their beautiful home by the sea in Cornwall, England, where I could complete this book in a tranquil environment. Then my heartfelt thanks to Paul Maisano for skillfully editing this book with diligence and care. Without Hisae Matsuda's careful consideration and sympathetic supervision in bringing all the necessary elements together, the project of this book would not have succeeded. So, I offer my wholehearted thanks to Hisae and everyone at Parallax Press for their help and support.

More broadly, I wish to thank the students and faculty members of Schumacher College where I have been developing the ideas of *Radical Love* during my Fireside Chats and other teaching sessions and informal conversations. Similarly, I thank the editors and readers of *Resurgence & Ecologist* magazine. Many of my ideas have evolved over the years while writing in the pages of the magazine. All our thriving is mutual, and all our work is cocreation. The book may carry my name, but the ideas and inspirations have come from many sources.

ABOUT THE AUTHOR

SATISH KUMAR, a former monk and long-term peace and environment activist, has been quietly setting the global agenda for change for more than fifty years. He was just nine when he left his family home to join the wandering Jains, and eighteen when he decided he could achieve more back in the world, campaigning for land reform in India and working to turn Gandhi's vision of a renewed India and a peaceful world into reality.

Inspired in his early twenties by the example of the British peace activist Bertrand Russell, Kumar embarked on an eight-thousand-mile peace pilgrimage. Carrying no money and depending on the kindness and hospitality of strangers, he and a colleague walked from India to America, via

Moscow, London, and Paris, to deliver a humble packet of "peace tea" to the leaders of the world's then four nuclear powers.

In 1973 Kumar settled in the UK, becoming the editor of *Resurgence* magazine (later known as *Resurgence & Ecologist*), a position he held until 2016, making him the UK's longest-serving editor of the same magazine. During this time, he has been the guiding spirit behind a number of now internationally respected ecological and educational ventures. He cofounded Schumacher College, an international center for ecological studies, where he continues to serve as a Visiting Fellow.

His autobiography, *No Destination,* first published by Green Books in 1978, has sold over fifty thousand copies. He is also the author of *You Are, Therefore I Am; The Buddha and the Terrorist; Earth Pilgrim; Soil, Soul, Society;* and *Elegant Simplicity: The Art of Living Well.*

He continues to teach and run workshops on reverential ecology, holistic education, and voluntary simplicity, and is a much sought-after speaker in the UK and internationally.

In 2022 Satish Kumar was awarded the Goi Peace Award in recognition of his lifelong dedication to campaigning for ecological regeneration, social justice, and spiritual fulfillment. Through his writings and educational activities, and as an embodiment of ecological and spiritual principles of living simply, he has inspired many people to transform themselves in order to transform the world.

Monastics and visitors practice the art of mindful living in the tradition of Thich Nhat Hanh at our mindfulness practice centers around the world. To reach any of these communities, or for information about how individuals, couples, and families can join in a retreat, please contact:

PLUM VILLAGE
33580 Dieulivol, France
plumvillage.org

LA MAISON DE L'INSPIR
77510 Villeneuve-sur-Bellot, France
maisondelinspir.org

HEALING SPRING
MONASTERY
77510 Verdelot, France
healingspringmonastery.org

MAGNOLIA GROVE
MONASTERY
Batesville, MS 38606, USA
magnoliagrovemonastery.org

BLUE CLIFF MONASTERY
Pine Bush, NY 12566, USA
bluecliffmonastery.org

DEER PARK MONASTERY
Escondido, CA 92026, USA
deerparkmonastery.org

EUROPEAN INSTITUTE OF
APPLIED BUDDHISM
D-51545 Waldbröl, Germany
eiab.eu

THAILAND PLUM VILLAGE
Nakhon Ratchasima
30130 Thailand
thaiplumvillage.org

ASIAN INSTITUTE OF
APPLIED BUDDHISM
Lantau Island, Hong Kong
pvfhk.org

STREAM ENTERING
MONASTERY
Beaufort, Victoria 3373
Australia
nhapluu.org

MOUNTAIN SPRING
MONASTERY
Bilpin, NSW 2758, Australia
mountainspringmonastery.org

For more information visit: *plumvillage.org*
To find an online sangha visit: *plumline.org*
For more resources, try the Plum Village app: *plumvillage.app*
Social media: *@thichnhathanh @plumvillagefrance*

THICH NHAT HANH FOUNDATION

planting seeds of Compassion

THE THICH NHAT HANH FOUNDATION works to continue the mindful teachings and practice of Zen Master Thich Nhat Hanh, in order to foster peace and transform suffering in all people, animals, plants, and our planet. Through donations to the Foundation, thousands of generous supporters ensure the continuation of Plum Village practice centers and monastics around the world, bring transformative practices to those who otherwise would not be able to access them, support local mindfulness initiatives, and bring humanitarian relief to communities in crisis in Vietnam.

By becoming a supporter, you join many others who want to learn and share these life-changing practices of mindfulness, loving speech, deep listening, and compassion for oneself, each other, and the planet.

For more information on how you can help support mindfulness around the world, or to subscribe to the Foundation's monthly newsletter with teachings, news, and global retreats, visit tnhf.org.

PARALLAX PRESS, a nonprofit publisher founded by Zen Master Thich Nhat Hanh, publishes books and media on the art of mindful living and Engaged Buddhism. We are committed to offering teachings that help transform suffering and injustice. Our aspiration is to contribute to collective insight and awakening, bringing about a more joyful, healthy, and compassionate society.

View our entire library at parallax.org.

THE MINDFULNESS BELL is a journal of the art of mindful living in the Plum Village tradition of Thich Nhat Hanh. To subscribe or to see the worldwide directory of Sanghas (local mindfulness groups), visit mindfulnessbell.org.